CHILD DEVELOPMENT
IN CONTEXT

CHILD DEVELOPMENT IN CONTEXT

Voices and Perspectives

David N. Sattler
College of Charleston

Geoffrey P. Kramer
Grand Valley State University
West Shore Community College

Virginia Shabatay
Palomar College

Douglas A. Bernstein
University of South Florida
University of Surrey

HOUGHTON MIFFLIN COMPANY   Boston   New York

Senior Sponsoring Editor: Kerry T. Baruth
Senior Associate Editor: Jane Knetzger
Editorial Assistant: Sarah Gessner
Senior Project Editor: Kathryn Dinovo
Senior Cover Design Coordinator: Deborah Azerrad Savona
Senior Manufacturing Coordinator: Sally Culler
Senior Marketing Manager: Pamela J. Laskey

Cover design: Rebecca Fagan
Cover images: Lori Adamski Peek/Tony Stone Images (top left); Photodisk (top right); Dale
Durfee/Tony Stone Images (bottom left); Andy Sacks/Tony Stone Images (bottom right)

Printed in the U.S.A.

Library of Congress Catalog Card Number: 99-71928

ISBN: 0-395-92103-1

1 2 3 4 5 6 7 8 9-CS-03 02 01 00 99

To my parents,
with deep respect and love
and
to my colleagues and friends, Norbert L. Kerr and Lawrence A. Messé

DAVID N. SATTLER

To my children, Rachel and Evan, who've made me the luckiest man
in the world

GEOFFREY P. KRAMER

To my beloved grandchildren, Nicole, Justin, and Phoenix,
who teach me to be happy for no particular reason

VIRGINIA SHABATAY

To Eleanor Bernstein, my mother and my friend

DOUGLAS A. BERNSTEIN

Brief Contents

Contents

1

BIRTH, INFANCY, AND TODDLERHOOD   1

> **Developmental Concepts:** reflexes, motor development, early object relations, language development, toilet training

Fascinated by his daughter Madeleine, a writer makes astute observations about the development of her motor skills, language, and imagination.

> **Developmental Concepts:** cross-cultural views of pregnancy and childbirth, gender preferences

When a woman announces that she is pregnant, the entire community in Quiche, Guatemala, prepares for the birth because the child will become the responsibility not only of its family but of all members of the village.

Mollie in Preschool   38

Vivian Gussin Paley

> **Developmental Concepts:** pretend play, preoperational period, peer relationships, symbolic thinking

> Three- and four-year-old children charm us as they engage in imaginative play and demonstrate developmental changes in memory and symbolic thinking.

Fantasy and Storytelling: Children at Play   43

Harry Crews

> **Developmental Concepts:** dramatic play, family and cultural influences

> Children use pictures from a catalog to tell stories that help them understand the drama of their lives.

Angela's Ashes: Memoir of a Childhood   48

Frank McCourt

> **Developmental Concepts:** poverty; family, community, and cultural factors influencing development

> A Pulitzer-Prize winner considers the effects of poverty, his father's alcoholism, and the expectations placed on him as a five-year-old.

Night Visitors: Imagination or Reality?   53

Annie Dillard

> **Developmental Concepts:** imagination, reality testing, problem solving

> A young child is captivated and frightened by shadows appearing in her bedroom but eventually comes to understand the source of her visions.

3

MIDDLE CHILDHOOD   63

The Spatial Child   81

John Philo Dixon

Developmental Concepts: special abilities, learning to read, motivation

The research director for the American Shakespeare Theater describes the negative effects of being told as a child that he had inadequate reading skills and of not discovering for several years his talents in mathematics.

Handed My Own Life   85

Annie Dillard

Developmental Concepts: industry, achievement, intrinsic motivation, extrinsic motivation, sense of self, curiosity

A noted writer remembers when her parents left her alone to discover the value of enjoying an activity for itself.

Helping Children Avoid Depression   88

Martin E. P. Seligman with Karen Reivich, Lisa Jaycox, and Jane Gillham

Developmental Concepts: childhood depression, coping skills, applied research

A team of research psychologists develops and assesses a program designed to teach coping strategies to fifth and sixth grade children who are at risk of depression.

4

ADOLESCENCE   95

Shaping Up Absurd   98

Nora Ephron

Developmental Concepts: physical development, body image, conformity

In a humorous vein, a noted writer and director recounts the humiliation she felt when she was slow to develop physically and became concerned that she did not meet certain standards of attractiveness.

Rinker Buck

> **Developmental Concepts:** sibling relationships, father-son relationships, initiative, individuation, independence
>
> At seventeen and fifteen years of age, two brothers become the youngest aviators to fly across America, and in the process learn more about themselves and each other than they expected.

Preface

Teaching child development is an inherently intellectual and emotional enterprise. As professors, we face the challenges of not only presenting theory and research clearly but also conveying our own involvement and excitement about the field. We want to show how what we study in the classroom relates to the world outside—in short, bring research and theory to life. Coupled with these challenges are other issues central to excellent teaching: (1) engaging students in critical thinking by having them reflect on and analyze difficult issues, such as disciplining and rewarding children, understanding how cognition changes over time, and recognizing how women and men at different stages balance autonomy and interdependence; and (2) exposing students to the complexities of life events, ethical dilemmas, and cross-cultural problems, such as raising a child in a single-parent family, learning the customs of a new country but retaining an identity with one's country of origin, and coping in midlife when confronted by pressures to assist children financially and to care for aging parents. We believe this book will help instructors create a dynamic learning environment and show students the vitality and complexity of the field of child development.

Our goals for *Child Development in Context: Voices and Perspectives* are the following:

- Promote understanding and retention of child development concepts and issues.

- Bring theory and research alive through dynamic and insightful first-person accounts and narratives that illustrate child development concepts and raise important and timely issues.

- Engage students in critical thinking about gender, multicultural, ethical, theoretical, and research issues.

- Expose students to the complexities of child development, life events, and ethical dilemmas.

- Broaden knowledge and awareness of the relationships among physical, cognitive, and psychosocial development.

This book can be used alone or in conjunction with any child development textbook.

Pedagogical Features

Each chapter contains five or six narratives written by popular and scholarly authors, and each narrative covers a different concept, issue, or topic within a given age period. Many narratives convey the complexities of child development by showing the relationships among the cognitive, physical, and psychosocial domains. To help provide a longitudinal perspective and illustrate developmental changes, we occasionally present more than one selection by a given author. Many selections highlight multicultural, gender, and ethical issues.

Each chapter and article begins with an introduction that orients the reader and presents the main child development concepts and issues that are illustrated in the reading. In addition, on the first page of each article we include a concept guide, in bold type, that lists the concepts and issues that the article illustrates. The concepts were selected after carefully reviewing more than a dozen of the best-selling child development textbooks and consulting with instructors who teach the course. Where possible, we provide brief biographical information about the author.

After each article, we include a series of questions designed to promote critical thinking and highlight research issues.

- The critical thinking questions, titled *Response and Analysis*, ask students to (1) reflect on and analyze the concepts and issues presented in the narrative, (2) connect material in the narrative with material presented in their main textbook or during lecture, (3) explore their own reactions to and experiences with the issues, and (4) apply the information (for example, propose an intervention program, outline recommendations for a local school board).

- The research questions, titled *Research*, provide a solid foundation for learning methodology at an introductory level. After briefly discussing a research study at a level appropriate for students who have not had a course in research methodology, we ask readers questions about how they might design the study, develop hypotheses, test alternative hypotheses, or interpret the results. The questions cover basic methodological concepts, such as identifying and measuring variables, controlling for extraneous variables, and applying ethical research principles. These questions show the importance of empirical research in understanding development. Students find these exercises interesting, in part because they involve issues raised in the readings.

Criteria for Selecting the Readings

We used several criteria to select the readings. First, each selection had to illustrate key concepts, issues, and topics that are presented in most child development textbooks. Second, and equally important, each narrative had to be provocative: It had to arouse us, hold our attention, raise questions, be of interest to students, and promote critical thinking. We favored selections that would broaden students' perspectives on gender, ethnic, and cultural influences. We included a few selections that cover non-normative aspects of development (for example, attention-deficit/hyperactivity disorder) because some instructors cover these topics in their course. Finally, we chose and edited selections so that they were long enough to be absorbing but short enough that instructors could easily assign them as supplemental readings.

Suggestions for the Instructor: How to Use This Book

Child Development in Context: Voices and Perspectives can be used to create an active learning environment in small and large classes. Instructors may assign the readings to correspond to material presented during lecture or in the primary textbook.

This book also can be used to promote class discussions and to develop research projects, writing assignments, and other individual or group projects.

Class Discussion

Students enjoy discussing their reactions to the readings in class.

1. The questions that follow each reading stimulate good class discussion and reinforce students' understanding of child development concepts. Instructors may ask students to answer the questions prior to or during the class and to share their responses with the class. This activity also can be a good way to introduce a topic in class.

    The research questions are an excellent resource for introducing and discussing research methodology. They address basic concepts and principles and underscore the importance of methodology and statistics to child development.

2. Students often enjoy a class debate. Many of the issues raised by the readings and the questions promote critical thinking and illustrate opposing viewpoints. For example, Richard Rodriguez's essay raises important questions concerning bilingualism. Should schools instruct children in their native language? How might the social and personal development of these children be affected by not learning well the language of their new country? What conflicts can occur in families when children adopt the customs of their new land? In another selection, LeAlan Jones and Lloyd Newman confront teenage pregnancy, racism, and poverty. How can we alleviate some of society's ills? How might citizens and government work together to eliminate drugs and guns from our homes and neighborhoods? How can we fight prejudice? Students may debate various sides of such issues in class.

Writing Assignments

Writing assignments allow students to analyze, question, and give personal responses to what they have read, and to develop writing skills. Instructors may require students to answer the questions for a given number of articles and to turn in their answers at assigned times during the course or at the end of the semester.

The readings and questions also can serve as a basis for journals or response papers. Instructors might allow students to develop ideas that occur to them after reading the narratives and questions. The writing assignments could also be turned in weekly or periodically throughout the course, depending on class size and time available to read and grade them. Instructors could assign grades, satisfactory or unsatisfactory credit, or extra credit as appropriate.

Research Projects

Instructors may use the readings to generate creative research projects.

1. Students could work alone or in groups to design a research proposal based on an idea raised in a reading or in the questions that follow each reading. The proposal might include (1) a statement of the problem or question and why it is interesting or important; (2) a summary of previous research exploring the problem or question; (3) a statement presenting the hypothesis, independent variable(s), and dependent variable(s); and (4) a description of the method (for example, participants, materials, procedures, controls, adherence to ethical standards).

2. Students could work alone or in groups to write a term paper based on one or several of the readings and could explore the current state of knowledge about the topic. The paper, which might include an introduction, a literature review, and a discussion, could be turned in during the term or presented in class in a ten-to-fifteen-minute presentation.

3. Advanced or honor students could investigate one question or author in detail. For instance, a student could read one or two books or articles by an author whose selection is included in this book. They could learn more about the political, social, and economic forces that might have affected the author or influenced the issue discussed in the reading. Students could submit a written research report or make an oral presentation to the class.

Group Projects

The readings can be used to generate engaging individual and group projects.

1. Students might work in small groups, and each student in the group could compare his or her responses to the questions. Instructors might provide a rough agenda and time limits. Each group might have a facilitator, recorder, and reporter. The group could compile and summarize its responses, and the reporter could present a synopsis to the class. The variability of responses both within and among groups is often instructive.

2. Students working in groups could identify links between concepts that are presented in other selections in the same chapter or in different chapters. For example, in the Birth, Infancy, and Toddlerhood chapter, Anne Lamott describes her son's growing curiosity and changing responses as he learns to crawl. In the Middle Childhood chapter, Annie Dillard learns the value of enjoying an activity for itself and not necessarily for the praise she receives from others. In the Adolescence chapter, Rinker Buck describes how he and his brother, both teenagers, planned and executed their cross-continental flight. All three articles

contain themes of autonomy, initiative, and self-sufficiency. Students could follow those themes through various ages, exploring how they are manifested differently and how maturational and situational factors influence their expression.

A Final Note: Extending the Borders

In his remarkable book *An Anthropologist on Mars*, Oliver Sacks tells us that he is best able to understand his patients when he gets out of his office and into their lives, making "house calls at the far borders of human experience." In this way he comes to know them and their conditions from within, as persons, and not merely as patients who have been handed a diagnosis. We believe that students, too, will better understand the issues in child development when they extend the borders of the theoretical into the world of human experience. We hope this book will help them do so.

Acknowledgments

It is a special pleasure to express our appreciation to the many talented and dedicated people who provided creative ideas and suggestions for this book. We thank Elaine Cassel (Marymount College, Lord Fairfax Community College) for her good counsel, and we thank the following individuals for reading various portions of the manuscript and offering constructive suggestions:

Ruth L. Ault, Davidson College
Lanthan D. Camblin, University of Cincinnati
Teresa K. Elliott, American University
Sharon B. Hamill, California State University–San Marcos
Amy J. Malkus, Washington State University
Herbert Merrill II, Erie Community College
Mary Kay Reed, York College of Pennsylvania

We have enjoyed working with the outstanding staff at Houghton Mifflin Company. Jane Knetzger, Senior Associate Editor, has provided invaluable support and advice on the structure of the book and pedagogy. She has been a strong advocate of this project and the *Psychology in Context* series. We thank Kerry T. Baruth, Senior Sponsoring Editor, and Sarah Gessner, Editorial Assistant, for their excellent support and professionalism. We thank Kathryn Dinovo, Senior Project Editor, for her excellent work in overseeing the production of this book; Craig Mertens for helping us secure permissions; and Melissa Lotfy of Books By Design for her assistance with production. We are grateful to Pamela Laskey, Marketing Manager, for her excitement about the book and creative ideas in promoting it. We also thank former Senior Sponsoring Editor David Lee, who originally signed the book, and Lou Gum, former Editorial Assistant, who provided valuable support.

We are indebted to Michael Phillips and the staff of the College of Charleston Interlibrary Loan Department and the staff of the Mason County Library in Ludington, Michigan, for helping us obtain books and other materials. Thanks also go to the staff of Palomar College in Escondido, California, and especially to Marcia Booth, whose gracious, invaluable help was given with great patience and a wonderful sense of humor. We thank Charles Kaiser, Conrad Festa, Samuel Hines, Stacy Clark, Dee Dee Luff, and the College of Charleston Department of Psychology faculty for their support.

We particularly wish to thank Yehuda Shabatay and Michelle King-Kramer for their steadfast enthusiasm toward this work, their ardent support, thorough reading of the manuscript, and their always valuable suggestions. We are indebted to Jerome M. Sattler for his wise counsel and unwavering support. Finally, we thank other family members: Heidi, Walter, Nicole, and Justin Philips; Bonnie and Keith Sattler; Debbie Hendrix; Rachael and Evan Kramer; Elizabeth, Tom, and Phoenix Voorhies; Deborah and Eli Knaan; Michael Shabatay; and Miss Lindsay N. Kennedy.

We always are delighted to hear from students and faculty who use the book. We especially welcome feedback on how to improve the book and suggestions for readings to include in the next edition.

David N. Sattler
College of Charleston
Department of Psychology
Charleston, South Carolina
E-mail: sattlerd@cofc.edu

Geoffrey P. Kramer
Department of Psychology
Grand Valley State University
Allendale, Michigan

Virginia Shabatay
Palomar College
Department of English
San Marcos, California

Douglas A. Bernstein
Department of Psychology
University of South Florida
Tampa, Florida
University of Surrey
Guildford, England

About the Authors

David N. Sattler is Associate Professor of Psychology at the College of Charleston. After graduating Phi Beta Kappa with a degree in psychology from San Diego State University, David received the M.A. and Ph.D. degrees in psychology from Michigan State University. He has held academic positions at the University of California at San Diego, San Diego State University, and Scripps College. His research examines behavior in social dilemmas, and coping, social support, family functioning, and posttraumatic stress disorder following natural disasters. He has published in numerous journals, including *Journal of Personality and Social Psychology*, *Journal of Applied Social Psychology*, *International Journal of Stress Management*, and *Teaching of Psychology*. He is an avid photographer and backpacker.

Geoffrey P. Kramer received the M.A. degree in clinical psychology with a minor in philosophy from Central Michigan University and the Ph.D. degree in psychology from Michigan State University. He teaches at Grand Valley State University and at West Shore Community College. Geoff previously held an academic position at Indiana University–Kokomo. He was a clinician for several years at the State Prison of Southern Michigan, and he also worked in private practice. His research interests and publications are primarily in the area of psychology and the law. In his leisure time, he enjoys spending time with his family, biking, playing tennis, reading, fishing, writing, and listening to music.

Virginia Shabatay received the Ph.D. degree in Humanities. She teaches at Palomar College in San Marcos, California, and has held academic positions at San Diego State University, Portland State University, Lewis and Clark College, and Grossmont College. She has served as editorial consultant on numerous books, including *Martin Buber's Life and Work* by Maurice Friedman, and she has contributed essays to several books. Her most recent publications are "Martin Buber and Sisela Bok: Against the Generation of the Lie," in *Martin Buber and the Human Sciences*, edited by Maurice Friedman, and "The Stranger: Who Calls? Who Answers?" in *Stories Lives Tell: Narrative and Dialogue in Education*, edited by Carol Witherell and Nel Noddings. In her leisure, she likes to read, travel, swim, and take long walks on the beach.

Douglas A. Bernstein received his undergraduate degree in psychology at the University of Pittsburgh in 1964, and the M.A. degree in psychology in 1966 and the Ph.D. degree in clinical psychology in 1968 from Northwestern University. He joined the faculty at the University of Illinois at Urbana-Champaign, where he holds the title of professor emeritus. Currently, he is Visiting Professor of Psychology at both the University of South Florida and the University of Surrey. His research interests have focused mainly on anxiety assessment and treatment, the modification of smoking behavior, and other topics in the field of behavioral medicine, but in recent years he has spent most of his time involved in promoting excellence in the teaching of psychology. This includes chairing program committees for the Annual National Institute on the Teaching of Psychology and the Annual American Psychological Society Preconvention Institute on the Teaching of Psychology, and writing and editing textbooks in introductory, clinical, abnormal, and applied psychology. His other interests include travel, reading, and rooting (in vain, it seems) for the Pittsburgh Steelers.

CHILD DEVELOPMENT
IN CONTEXT

BIRTH, INFANCY, AND TODDLERHOOD

One time, when I was little more than a baby, I was taken to visit my grandmother, who was living in a cottage on a nearly uninhabited stretch of beach in northern Florida. I remember of this visit being picked up from my crib in what seemed the middle of the night and carried from my bedroom and out of doors, where I had my first look at the stars.

It must have been an unusually clear and beautiful night for someone to have said, "Let's wake the baby and show her the stars."

MADELEINE L'ENGLE, *Glimpses of Grace*

What adult has not wondered about the psychological life of the youngest humans? What do infants think about? What do they know? Of what are they conscious? Using new methods of observation, researchers have found that babies have a much broader array of knowledge and skills than they are usually given credit for. A newborn's reflexes, vocalizations, and expressions help ensure survival and promote attachments to caretakers. Within the first few months, babies quickly develop complex understandings of the world around them. They rapidly develop social and interpersonal skills. By age two, most children are effective communicators who know perhaps one hundred or two hundred words and can speak two- or three-word sentences.

The readings in this section convey the wondrous speed with which development occurs. Writer Brian Hall describes his daughter, Madeleine, at different stages during her first two years. Madeleine is born with the basic repertoire of reflexes common to all human infants, but she quickly sharpens her perceptual and physical abilities. By the time she is six months old, she has begun to utter monosyllables such as *da, ma,* or *gn.* As Madeleine begins her second year, Hall looks for indications that she has started using imaginative play. When Madeleine puts a baby doll on the floor and says to her parents, "Shh," is she merely imitating someone or has she begun to engage in make believe? She has begun to show imagination, autonomy, and self-regulation, all skills she will put to greater use in early childhood.

Rigoberta Menchú reminds us that different cultures vary in their beliefs and practices concerning childbirth. A Mayan native of Guatemala, Menchú describes how, once a woman is pregnant, the expected child is presumed to belong to the whole community. She also describes the ways in which the child is inaugurated into the community and the community is introduced to the child. How do the practices she describes differ from those in the United States?

Not all infants are fortunate to have good health and supportive environments. Pediatricians T. Berry Brazelton and Bertrand Cramer describe the case of Clarissa, a baby born at only twenty-seven weeks gestational age. Worldwide, about one newborn in seven is born preterm, with the highest rates of prematurity occurring in poorer countries. Preterm and low-birth-weight babies have a higher risk of illness, both immediately after birth and later. They generally are also less responsive than full-term babies and require nearly constant care, which puts a considerable strain on parents. Brazelton and Cramer describe how Clarissa, who weighed only two pounds at birth, was able to survive, thanks to advances in medical care and to her parents' persistent love.

All babies present challenges for parents, and William and Martha Sears's daughter, Hayden, is no exception. Hayden was a demanding baby with a temperament very different from those of her siblings. Her parents describe feeling at the mercy of their child's needs and learning to change their style of parenting to adapt to those needs. The Sears show that parents who are flexible and able to respond to a child's individuality can have a positive long-term effect on their children.

The final selection illustrates how sensorimotor development is intimately tied to cognitive and emotional development. Anne Lamott's son, Sam, seems to understand that objects put out of sight continue to exist—a critical milestone in Piaget's theory of cognitive development—but his understanding seems tenuous and uncertain. As he learns to crawl, Sam interacts much more confidently with the environment. He anticipates objects in familiar rooms and shows surprise when something in the room is different. He gets a gleam in his eye and picks up and then drops or throws each item he finds. These behaviors suggest important changes in Sam's cognitive relations with the world.

MADELEINE'S FIRST MONTHS OF LIFE

Brian Hall

Developmental Concepts
reflexes, motor development, early object relations,
language development, toilet training

Brian Hall, a devoted and loving father, is enchanted with his newborn daughter, Madeleine. Madeleine comes into the world with the basic reflexes and abilities needed to survive. What can she hear and how well can she see, Hall wonders. As Madeleine continues to grow, Hall is fascinated by the ways in which she interacts with objects and her world. Does she understand that the objects still exist even though she can no longer see them? As Madeleine grows, she enjoys playing games such as peekaboo and exchanging toys and other objects with her parents; for her father, these games are social and represent the beginnings of communication. Her communication skills increase markedly, and she begins to show signs of imagination and creativity.

Reflexes Soon After Birth

Madeleine was born just past midnight. The room had been heated to eighty degrees, so it would not have felt cold, but what a chilling void it must have seemed. . . .

Laid on Pamela,[1] . . . she churned her arms and legs [near] the breast. She . . . chomped down on the nipple. . . . Nothing came out. But perhaps she didn't know anything was supposed to come out; she knew only that she must suck. . . .

What could she hear? Water remains in the newborn's ear, easing the transition to the sharper sounds outside the womb. She could probably already recognize Pamela's voice, and perhaps mine. . . .

How well could she see? Not across the room, not to the door through which one of the midwives was hurrying toward the telephone. A newborn can focus between eight and ten inches away, the distance from breast to face. Adrenaline grants

---

[1]Pamela: Madeleine's mother.

her an hour or so of alertness and calm, a heightened awareness that will not return for days, and this is the window celebrated in recent years as an opportunity to bond with the maternal face, the one clear image in the little circle beyond which vague shapes flutter and murmur. . . .

As for Madeleine's point of view, one can only guess, in the first weeks, at the mix of volition and reflex. Placed on her stomach, she "swam," kicking her legs and flailing her arms. Attagirl! I might think, or I might hurry to relieve her of what could be distress. But all newborns do this automatically. . . . Is it a dying remnant of life in the womb? Or a much deeper genetic signpost, pointing back to our ancient aquatic existence?

She would grasp anything that touched her palm and be unable to let go. Look at newborn monkeys, developmentalists say, who must grip their mothers' hair to ride on their backs. A human newborn has such a strong grip she can hang from a bar. You might think the purpose of that startling hard squeeze on your index finger is to strengthen the grip even more, but in fact it's getting weaker by the day.

In the so-called Moro reflex, a newborn who thinks she is falling will shoot out both hands, spreading fingers to clutch at the air, and then pull her arms tight against her chest. An idea almost inevitably intrudes: branches! The hairy, pea-brained, pre-australopithecine babe is falling out of the tree and it spastically spreadeagles to catch branches in its strong grip. If a human baby, in falling, happens to be holding a pencil in one hand, only her other hand will shoot out. Evidently, she thinks the pencil is a branch. But if the baby is holding her thumbs, this satisfies her as well as the pencil does, and neither hand reaches out.

The swimming reflex, the grasp, the Moro—all are remnants, somewhat mysterious, of larger urges and larger questions spanning eons and species, out of which the baby sails. They disappear before our eyes as she individualizes, as she slowly coalesces out of Life into her own life.

It was in the nursing that Pamela and I got our earliest sense of Madeleine as an individual, as something more than a mere bundle of irrepressible urges. When we compared her with the babies of our friends (all of whom seemed to be having babies at the same time we did; or did we just lose our other friends?), she seemed by far the most avid nurser. She had an idiosyncratic way of attaching. She would dart her head forward and fasten on the nipple with a sudden bite, vigorously shaking her head. . . . Later, when the rooting reflex abated and she was capable of turning away from the nipple after a couple of sucks to see what else was going on, she seemed partly to do this because it allowed her to start again with another . . . bite and shake. . . .

Early Relations with the Environment

When I first held Madeleine up to a mirror, she ignored her own reflection and stared at mine. I tried to direct her attention to her image, but she merely glanced at my pointing finger and back at me. At this stage she took in everything with the same wide, bright-blank eyes, all reception and no transmission, so interest could be gauged only by the length of time she stared at an object. My face was noteworthy and hers was not, which suggested to me that she already could recognize my face, and in the confused swirl of her world settled on it as a familiar island. Perhaps she also knew that engagement with this face brought results, like getting picked up and carried to the breast. . . .

At around two months, she began to prefer her own reflection in the mirror to mine. Perhaps she had now grown familiar with her own face and liked its simpler, more ideal features, its exaggerated eyes. Or perhaps it was still less familiar to her than my face, but as the world around her grew less intimidating, she was beginning to prefer novelty. Certainly her interests were expanding beyond mere faces (love me!) and breasts (feed me!), as she perhaps began to assume the bare fact of her survival and wondered what else there might be. . . .

Among her earliest possessions was a small yellow terry-cloth duck with a printed wing of blazing red. That wing fascinated her. It was so bright it seemed to float off the body of the duck. She would arch her back in the fold-up travel bassinet that was her bed for the first four months and stare up at the red wing in the corner.

One morning I was peering in at that avid stare. Something momentous was happening. Her right arm was twitching. It jigged her hand up and flapped it down again. The hand fluttered at the end of the questing arm like a fish on a line, struggling but unable to control where it would be yanked next. It fetched up against the cloth side of the bassinet and stuck there. The autonomous wrist joined the fray and commenced wiping the hand up and down the wall in an attempt to drag it free. When this maneuver succeeded, the force of the effort shot the arm above the head. Madeleine arched her back farther and focused again on the wing. The arm jerked. The hand whipsawed. It fell short and far, like artillery finding its range. At last it glanced off the duck, nudging it out of reach. The arm lay still and the hand softly flexed and unflexed, as though gasping for breath.

Interaction! Agency! Surely our hands are our most important discovery before speech. Madeleine was no longer a passive viewer, a mere receptacle. The world was different for her being in it. *She had moved the red wing.* And a more profound discovery was now possible. She and the world were distinct from each other. Her hands—these fascinating wiggly objects that floated into her field of vision even more often than the face with the breasts and the other one with the arms—could be commanded. They, like the two obedient faces, apparently belonged to her. The red wing did not. It would not move until the hand touched it. And when the hand did touch it, Madeleine could see the boundary of self: Madeleine touched not-Madeleine. . . .

A pointed finger became a concrete manifestation of the attention Madeleine could focus on not-Madeleine. Bending low over the tray of her highchair, she would fix her gaze on a stray droplet of juice and lower her index finger onto it with excruciating care. She would not so much probe the drop as hold it down. Looking at us, she would solemnly raise that finger and guide it into the line between her eyes and ours, as though commanding us, too, to stay where we were. . . .

Globes and circles retained their importance, but now a whole new class of objects in the house called to her. Drawer handles that flipped up and fell back down. Pot lids that turned over with a cowbell clank. And best of all, doors. To a baby not yet strong enough to lift an orange, these were an amazement, as a single swipe transformed a whole wall. . . .

From here it was a short step to handing objects to us. Partly this was imitative, since as far as she could tell, the point of our existence was mainly to hand objects to her. Partly it was reassuring, like peekaboo, which appeared at around this time (six months). In peekaboo, the parental face does the worst thing it can do: it disappears. But a few seconds later it pops back, and the child's relief bubbles up in a giggle. When Madeleine raised her dress above her head and waited for us to sing out, "Where's Madeleine?," precipitating a downward fling on "There she is!," it was not she who was hiding, but the whole world, and what reassurances later in life could match that budding realization that the cosmos did not need her constant vigilance to continue existing? . . .

First Use of Language

For Madeleine, immersion in language began in rituals of rhythm and song. . . . Madeleine's first sound of my voice was a bad Placido Domingo, crooning "Un Dì Felice" through the uterine wall. Later, Pamela rocked her to sleep with lullabies: "I Gave My Love a Cherry," "Shenandoah." I preferred pacing to rocking, and ballads to lullabies: "Barbara Allen," "Henry Martin." . . .

But songs were only a fraction of it. Virtually every time I spoke to Madeleine I used a voice that seems to come unbidden to parents, a rhythmic, rhyming chant, as though I were summoning her spirit or coaxing a new one out of myself. The altered cadence must be useful to the infant, a signal that these words, hopping and bopping out of the background chatter, are meant for her. I found myself speculating about this one day after I had spent five minutes bouncing Madeleine in my arms and asking her, in a dotted rhythm arranged in bars of 2/4: "Who's this little | ba-by with the | stuffed-up | nose?" . . .

I thought more about this when Madeleine began to speak in clear syllables. All over the world, babies begin with the same basic repertory of utterances. This initial vocabulary, reasonably enough, consists of the easiest sounds to produce: the vowel sound *ah*; the labial consonants *p*, *b*, and *m*; and the tongue taps *t* and *d*. It is no coincidence that the core family words "mama," "baba," "papa," "dada," and "tata," which occur throughout the world, are constructed out of these sounds. But individual babies vary as to which of these sounds they use most, and Madeleine's preference was unequivocal: "Da!" . . .

Madeleine's next step was to discover that vocalization—this stick with which she tapped objects, or beat out a rhythm to beat back not-Madeleine—could also be used to communicate, as her hands, in waving, were learning to do. Perhaps it made sense, then, that her first understanding of the call-and-response possibilities of sound seemed to come in conjunction with the hand. When Pamela, one day, hummed to her while dribbling an index finger over her lips, Madeleine picked it up almost immediately. Now, from across a room, she could make me stop whatever I was doing to wave to her with one hand and dribble my lips with the other. . . .

At six months, Madeleine loved this: I would touch my head to hers and sing a tone. She, wide-eyed, concentrating, would match it. The tone would vibrate through both our heads. I would nudge my pitch up or down and a pulse would begin, as the two nearly identical sound waves throbbed in and out of phase. Madeleine, imitating me, would adjust her note as well. If we eased the pitches further apart the pulse quickened into a blur, if we brought them back toward each other it slowed, to a run, a walk, a wary standstill. Everything was combined here: pitch, rhythm, communication, touch. The slow pulse in our heads was like the heartbeat in the womb, that first muscle of that first sphere, but this was music of two spheres, social instead of solipsistic, the rhythm in each impossible without the other. We were there.

Development of Imagination

I had been watching out for the beginnings of make-believe ever since her first birthday. . . .

Madeleine as a baby had been awash in wild imaginings, delusions, projected fears. [Eventually] she began to grasp . . . what was real and what was not. . . .

At fourteen months she pushed a wooden car around the floor and said "Brrm!" Aha! I thought. But once again, the evidence was tainted. When I had first given her the car, I had pushed it around myself and said "Brrm." (All self-respecting researchers, throw up your hands.) It occurred to me to wonder if I was viewing the learning process backward, anyway. I had assumed that she would eventually accomplish the conceptual leap from toy car to real car, and that she would then express that understanding by making the toy car act like a real car. But perhaps it went the other way around: I gave her the wooden car; she had no idea it represented the large object in our driveway; I moved it around, saying "Brrm"; she imitated me; after several days or weeks of making the little wooden thing act like a car, she gradually came to associate it with the real car. Body taught mind, rather than vice versa. Rote learning was absorbed until it became indistinguishable from insight.

She hugged her stuffed animals, but that didn't mean she was pretending they were alive, since she also hugged pillows and fluffy balls. . . . One of her cows mooed when it was turned over, and her reaction of anxious surprise suggested she knew perfectly well the thing wasn't alive and she didn't appreciate it pretending otherwise. . . .

At sixteen months, Madeleine was with us in a toy store when she spotted a two-year-old boy holding a doll. This doll was only six inches long, with an almost spherical head, full cheeks, and wide-open blue eyes. . . . It could not have looked more like Madeleine if it had been modeled on her. . . . Madeleine carried Bald Baby everywhere. Her small cloth body was easy to hold in one hand, and Madeleine enjoyed an occasional contemplative suck on the smooth round head of soft plastic (which made her look a bit unnervingly like Kronos eating his own children). With a good deal of tugging and tweezering finger work, Bald Baby's sleeper was removable, and the only thing Madeleine liked better than putting it on was taking it off again. I assumed off always eventually won out over on, because it felt more intimate to Madeleine, more secure. She had probably already come to associate underwear or nakedness with home, and in the coming months would strip all her favorite dolls as far as she could. Bald Baby, lying around in her unremovable underwear, was not only clearly a good friend of ours, she also was evidently not about to go anywhere.

During Madeleine's baths, in the big tub with me or Pamela, Bald Baby sat on the rim and watched, and was later dropped into the plastic tub, pulled out, dropped again. Before Madeleine ate, she stuffed Bald Baby into the mouth of an upright cardboard cylinder (part of a building set) so that only the doll's head, arms, and feet stuck out. "Hai-ch'," Madeleine explained. Highchair. Apparently, Bald Baby functioned somewhat like a voodoo doll in reverse. Instead of causing thing to happen to Madeleine, she confirmed what had already happened. Not only could Madeleine look from her own highchair to Bald Baby on hers and think, "I am here, I am eating," but she could do to Bald Baby what we did to Madeleine. Of her several incorporations, this internalization of authority was perhaps the most important to her self-constructing sense of self. Certainly it was the one she would practice most assiduously, or rather, compulsively, in the months to come. (When she learns the word, perhaps she will call it her conscience.)

Naturally I couldn't know whether Madeleine had really just made a conceptual breakthrough or had merely progressed physically to the point where I could infer her thoughts from her actions. Whichever was the case, soon after I noticed her breathing life into her dolls, I saw her do it to other things. Perhaps it had taken a mirror image to unlock her empathy, but once unlocked, empathy obeyed its own logic and flowed everywhere. She pushed raisins around on her highchair tray, saying "Brrm," and I wondered whether she was imagining they were cars, like the one in our driveway, or wheeled wooden blocks, like the one she had in her toy chest, or both. She jumped the raisins over little puddles of milk, and here I recognized a moment from a book we had just read, in which two rabbits were jumping over daisies.

Increasing Autonomy and Use of Language

Madeleine's words at nineteen months sketched out a portrait of Madeleine's world, a guide to what was important to her.

"Ba-bö" was diaper. When I opened hers up, if there was poop I bugged out my eyes and dropped my jaw the way I did when I saw her tummy, and I announced "Poop!" and she joyfully shouted "Poop!" and rocked back, flinging up her legs to hold her feet. "Wawa" was the water in the cup, and "bukreh" was one of the wiping cloths. . . . With her new diaper on, Madeleine flushed the toilet herself, waving her poop goodbye. . . .

Madeleine would hold Bald Baby up to me and say "Poop!" . . . "Ba-bö—*aw!*" Diaper—*off!* Madeleine's make-believe had now become sophisticated enough that she didn't always need a prop (although she preferred one), and she accepted from my hand motions that I was removing an invisible diaper, bugging my eyes out at [its] contents, sloughing them into an invisible toilet, flushing and waving goodbye. If I tried to put on a new diaper immediately, Madeleine objected, "Bukreh!," and I had to back up, wipe Bald Baby's butt, dry her off, apply some oil. "Ba-bö—*aw!*" Diaper—*on!* I would mime it and hand Bald Baby over with a silent prayer. But usually in vain. "Poop!" Madeleine would announce, handing her back. (The fact that she used "aw" to mean both "on" and "off" facilitated another self-perpetuating game: she was interested in the putting on and taking off of her shoes, and could simply shout "Aw!" at me continually as I went through a number of cycles.) . . .

"Ch'" meant chair. Chairs loomed large in Madeleine's mind as the loci of important activities. "Hai-ch'" was where she ate. "Aunh-ch'" (armchair) was where she looked at books with us during the day. "Raw-ch'" (rocking chair) was where we read in the evenings and sang to her. She had measured her physical progress in terms of chairs. Back in her crawling days, her instinctual urge to climb had sent her repeatedly up into her own miniature chair, where she would get stuck, straddling the summit. Later she drafted the full-size chairs into service as makeshift walkers, and pushed them shuddering around the house. Now that she could climb into the rocking chair, we often found her there, blissed out on the motion. We bought a rocking horse, which she also loved, and also called "raw-ch'." . . .

She now had the core family words well in hand. At eighteen months, she had switched from "Dada" to "Daddy," as the months of evidence from her ears finally penetrated that inner sanctum of preverbal utterances. Pamela remained "Mama," since that was the word we used. "Baby" had multiple uses. Bald Baby was "baby," and so was Big Baby. Real babies were baby. A small version of some familiar object, such as an undersized vegetable, was baby. . . .

The most important meaning of "baby" was this particular baby, Madeleine. She knew that folding her arm back toward herself meant "This is me," so for extra emphasis, just to make sure, she folded it as tight as she could and stuck her index finger in her armpit, her elbow bobbing like a chicken wing: "Baby!" Now that she had a clear word for herself, and a percussive one at that, she wielded it like a baseball bat, asserting her will. If I handed her a cracker, she flapped her arms in desperate disapproval and rained *b*'s down on me, boxing my ears, "Baby! Baby!"— meaning that baby must get the cracker out of the bag herself. This demand was not merely to show me, and herself, that she was physically capable of reaching into the bag, but to exercise choice. Confronted constantly with her own powerlessness—carried wherever Pamela or I needed to go, eating what we gave her, unable to do this and forced to do that for unfathomable reasons—naturally she needed to exercise power in the tiny areas allowed her. At this age, alas, those were often areas in which her choice not only didn't matter, but *obviously* didn't matter, yet she had learned how to pretend, and make-believe is the toddler's therapy, so by God she would pretend, and believe, that the choice was crucial, that the world hung on it. Baby certainly did not want *that* cracker. What on earth did I take her for? Ahh, yes, *this* one . . . bliss)!

Response and Analysis

1. What primitive reflexes does Madeleine exhibit soon after her birth? What other reflexes do newborns have that Brian Hall does not mention? Hall speculates about the origins and purposes of her reflexes. What are Hall's ideas? Do you agree with them? Why or why not?

2. Madeleine shows many signs of acquiring language as a young infant. How variable is children's language acquisition? Specifically, what is the difference between the number of words a child understands and the number of words a child produces at the age of twelve months? At the age of eighteen months? At the age of twenty-four months?

3. Hall distinguishes between imitation and imaginative play. Is this a useful distinction? Why or why not? How might the ability to imitate versus to create make-believe situations reflect differences in cognitive development? According to developmental psychologists, at what age do children begin to imitate others? At what age do children begin engaging in make-believe?

4. Bowel and bladder training are important developmental milestones. What physical, cognitive, and emotional factors influence the success of toilet training? How might parents' reactions to their children's successes and failures contribute to children's feelings of autonomy versus feelings of shame and doubt?

Research

Suppose you have developed a program to improve parenting skills, and you are now designing a study to assess its effectiveness. One group of parents watches a series of one-hour videotapes of experts discussing parenting skills. They watch these in their own homes once a week for four weeks. A second group discusses their parenting problems and concerns with a group leader one hour a week for four weeks. At the end of the four-week period, the participants rate how helpful they believe the program was to them, and they complete a survey asking how they might react to various parenting situations. What is (are) the independent variable(s)? How many levels or conditions of independent variable(s) are there? What are the levels or conditions? What is the dependent variable? Which program do you think parents would rate as more helpful? Why?

BIRTH CEREMONIES OF THE QUICHE COMMUNITY

Rigoberta Menchú

Developmental Concepts
cross-cultural views of pregnancy and childbirth,
gender preferences

Rigoberta Menchú grew up in a poor peasant village in Guatemala. In this selection, Menchú details the ways in which not only the parents but the entire Quiche community prepares for a birth. As soon as a pregnancy is made public, the expected infant is given the protective care of selected members of the community. The expectant mother prepares the child for this world even before it is born. After its birth, there are designated periods where the child is introduced to various obligations expected of it as a member of the community.

In our community there is an elected representative, someone who is highly respected. He's not a king but someone whom the community looks up to like a father. In our village, my father and mother were the representatives. Well, then the whole community becomes the children of the woman who's elected. So a mother, on her first day of pregnancy, goes with her husband to tell these elected leaders that she's going to have a child, because the child will not only belong to them but to the whole community and must follow as far as he can our ancestors' traditions. The leaders then pledge the support of the community and say: "We will help you, we will be the child's second parents." They are known as *abuelos*, "grandparents" or "forefathers." The parents then ask the "grandparents" to help them find the child some godparents, so that if he's orphaned, he shouldn't be tempted by any of the bad habits our people sometimes fall into. So the "grandparents" and the parents choose the godparents together. It's also the custom for the pregnant mother's neighbors to visit her every day and take her little things, no matter how simple. They stay and talk to her, and she'll tell them all her problems.

Later, when she's in her seventh month, the mother introduces her baby to the natural world, as our customs tell her to. She goes out in the fields or walks over the hills. She also has to show her baby the kind of life she leads, so that if she gets up at three in the morning, does her chores and tends the animals, she does it all the more so when she's pregnant, conscious that the child is taking all this in. She talks to the child continuously from the first moment he's in her stomach, telling him how hard his life will be. It's as if the mother were a guide explaining things to a tourist. She'll say, for instance, "You must never abuse nature and you must live your life as honestly as I do." As she works in the fields, she tells her child all the little things about her work. It's a duty to her child that a mother must fulfill. And then, she also has to think of a way of hiding the baby's birth from her other children.

When her baby is born, the mother mustn't have her other children around her. The people present should be the husband, the village leaders, and the couple's parents. . . .

The purity with which the child comes into the world is protected for eight days. Our customs say that the newborn baby should be alone with his mother in a special place for eight days, without any of her other children. Her only visitors are the people who bring her food. This is the baby's period of integration into the family; he very slowly becomes a member of it. When the child is born, they kill a sheep and there's a little fiesta just for the family. Then the neighbors start coming to visit and bring presents. They either bring food for the mother or something for the baby. The mother has to taste all the food her neighbors bring to show her appreciation for their kindness. After the eight days are over, the family counts up how many visitors the mother had and how many presents were received; things like eggs or food apart from what was brought for the mother, or clothing, small animals, and wood for the fire, or services like carrying water and chopping wood. If, during the eight days, most of the community has called, this is very important, because it means that this child will have a lot of responsibility toward his community when he grows up. The community takes over all the household expenses for these eight days and the family spends nothing.

After eight days, everything has been received, and another animal is killed as recognition that the child's right to be alone with his mother is over. All the mother's clothes, bedclothes, and everything she used during the birth are taken away by our elected leader and washed. She can't wash them in the well, so no matter how far away the river is, they must be carried and washed there. The baby's purity is washed away and he's ready to learn the ways of humanity. The mother's bed is moved to a part of the house which has first been washed with water and lime. Lime is sacred. It strengthens the child's bones. I believe this really is true. It gives a child strength to face the world. The mother has a bath in the *temascal* and puts on clean clothes. Then the whole house is cleaned. The child is also washed and dressed and put into the new bed. Four candles are placed on the corners of the bed to represent the four corners of the house and show him that this will be his home. They symbolize the respect the child must have for his community, and the responsibility he must feel toward it as a member of a household. The candles are lit and give off an incense which incorporates the child into the world he must live in. When the baby is born, his hands and feet are bound to show him that they are sacred and must only be used to work or do whatever nature meant them to do. They must never steal or abuse the natural world, or show disrespect for any living thing.

After the eight days, his hands and feet are untied and he's now with his mother in the new bed. This means he opens the doors to the other members of the community, because neither the family nor the community know him yet. Or rather, they weren't shown the baby when he was born. Now they can all come and kiss him. The neighbors bring another animal, and there's a big lunch in the new baby's house for all the community. This is to celebrate his integration "in the universe," as our parents used to say. Candles will be lit for him, and his candle becomes part of the candle of the whole community, which now has one more person, one more member. The whole community is at the ceremony, or at least, if not all of it, then some of it. Candles are lit to represent all the things which belong to the universe—earth, water, sun, and man—and the child's candle is put with them, together with incense (what we call *pom*) and lime—our sacred lime. Then the parents tell the baby of the suffering of the family he will be joining. With great feeling, they express their sorrow at bringing a child into the world to suffer. To us, suffering is our fate, and the child must be introduced to the sorrows and hardship, but he must learn that despite his suffering, he will be respectful and live through his pain. The child is then entrusted with the responsibility for his community and told to abide by its rules. After the ceremony comes the lunch, and then the neighbors go home. Now there is only the baptism to come.

When the baby is born, he's given a little bag with a garlic, a bit of lime, salt, and tobacco in it to hang round his neck. Tobacco is important because it is a sacred plant for Indians. This all means that the child can ward off all the evil things in life. For us, bad things are like spirits, which exist only in our imagination. Something bad, for instance, would be if the child were to turn out to be a gossip—not sincere, truthful, and respectful, as a child should be. It also helps him collect together and preserve all our ancestors' things. That's more or less the idea of the bag—to keep him pure. The bag is put inside the four candles as well, and this represents the promise of the child when he grows up.

When the child is forty days old, there are more speeches, more promises on his behalf, and he becomes a full member of the community. This is his baptism. All the important people of the village are invited and they speak. The parents make a commitment. They promise to teach the child to keep the secrets of our people, so that our culture and customs will be preserved. The village leaders come and offer their experience, their example, and their knowledge of our ancestors. They explain how to preserve our traditions. Then, they promise to be responsible for the child, teach him as he grows up, and see that he follows in their ways. It's also something of a criticism of humanity, and of the many people who have forsaken their traditions. They say almost a prayer, asking that our traditions again enter the spirits of those who have forsaken them. Then, they evoke the names of our ancestors, like Tecun Umán and others who form part of the ceremony, as a kind of chant. They must be remembered as heroes of the Indian peoples. . . .

When little girls are born, the midwives pierce their ears at the same time as they tie their umbilical cords. The little bags around their necks and the thread used to tie their umbilical cord are both red. Red is very significant for us. It means heat, strength, all living things. It's linked to the sun, which for us is the channel to the one God, the heart of everything, of the universe. So red gives off heat and fire, and red things are supposed to give life to the child. At the same time, it asks him to respect living things too. There are no special clothes for the baby. We don't buy anything special beforehand but just use pieces of *corte*[1] to wrap him in.

When a male child is born, there are special celebrations, not because he's male but because of all the hard work and responsibility he'll have as a man. It's not that *machismo* doesn't exist among our people, but it doesn't present a problem for the community because it's so much part of our way of life. The male child is given an extra day alone with his mother. The usual custom is to celebrate a male child by killing a sheep or some chickens. Boys are given more, they get more food because their work is harder and they have more responsibility. At the same time, he is head of the household, not in the bad sense of the word, but because he is responsible for so many things. This doesn't mean girls aren't valued. Their work is hard too and there are other things that are due to them as mothers. Girls are valued because they are part of the earth, which gives us maize, beans, plants, and everything we live on. The earth is like a mother which multiplies life. So the girl child will multiply the life of our generation and of our ancestors whom we must respect. The girl and the boy are both integrated into the community in equally important ways; the two are interrelated and compatible. Nevertheless, the community is always happier when a male child is born and the men feel much prouder. The customs, like the tying of the hands and feet, apply to both boys and girls.

Babies are breast-fed. It's much better than any other sort of food. But the important thing is the sense of community. It's something we all share. From the very first day, the baby belongs to the community, not only to the parents, and the baby must learn from all of us. . . . In fact, we behave just like bourgeois families in that, as soon as the baby is born, we're thinking of his education, of his well-being. But our people feel that the baby's school must be the community itself, that he must learn to live like all the rest of us. The tying of the hands at birth also symbolizes this; that no one should accumulate things the rest of the community does not have and he must know how to share, to have open hands. The mother must teach the baby to be generous. This way of thinking comes from poverty and suffering. Each child is taught to live like the fellow members of his community.

---

[1]*corte:* multicolored material that Guatemalan women use as a skirt. It is part of their traditional costume.

Response and Analysis

1. According to Rigoberta Menchú, how does the Quiche community support parents during pregnancy, prepare for a new baby, and take care of an infant? How do other family members, including children, help raise a newborn? How is the approach of the Quiche community similar to and different from the approach in your community?

2. Menchú describes practices such as isolating the mother and newborn infant for eight days, placing candles at the corners of the baby's bed, and binding the newborn's hands and feet for eight days. According to Menchú, what is the purpose of these practices? What do you think about them? What practices concerning childbirth within your own culture might be regarded by persons from other cultures as symbolic, ritualistic, or unusual? Why?

3. How might a culture's emphasis on characteristics such as independence, obedience, and physical intimacy influence (a) the way parents raise their children and (b) the traits that children develop? What evidence might support or dispute the influence of culture on (a) the way parents raise their children and (b) the traits that children develop?

Research

Suppose you are interested in studying the relationship between physical contact between parents and their young children and self-esteem in the children. You want to know how the amount of physical contact with parents correlates with self-esteem in children. Do you expect that physical contact will correlate with self-esteem? Why or why not? Imagine that your findings show that physical contact is positively correlated with self-esteem. Based on this finding, could you conclude that physical contact produces higher self-esteem in children? Why or why not? What other factors might explain this finding?

CARING FOR A PREMATURE INFANT

T. Berry Brazelton and Bertrand G. Cramer

Developmental Concepts
premature birth, primitive reflexes, attachment,
parental expectations, parent-child interactions

Clarissa was born at twenty-seven weeks gestational age and weighed only two pounds. During the first months of life, premature infants may sleep longer but cry and fuss more often than infants delivered at full term. These babies may be less responsive and alert; may have less physical contact such as touching and cuddling with their parents; and are more likely to develop allergies, respiratory problems, and other physical ailments. However, by the time they reach kindergarten, most children born prematurely are likely to match the physical and mental abilities of their peers who were born full term. In this selection, Drs. Brazelton and Cramer describe Clarissa's premature birth and development during her first year. What problems does Clarissa have? What care has helped in her development? How did the hospital staff guide and encourage her parents?

Clarissa D. was born prematurely to a thirty-one-year-old mother who had had several miscarriages. . . .

She went into labor at twenty-seven weeks . . . and the two-pound baby was delivered. The infant survived despite many complications. She was in severe distress with Apgar scores[1] of 5 at one minute, 7 at five minutes, requiring oxygen for resuscitation. Respiratory distress ensued and, for seven weeks, Clarissa was given constant artificial respiratory support with a tube in her throat and numerous medications. . . . She required pulmonary surgery and developed an infection and pneumonia, for which she received antibiotics for fourteen days. Despite all of these complications, Clarissa survived and was placed in room air at the age of

---

[1]Apgar score: a system to evaluate the general physical health of a newborn infant. An Apgar score is based on five factors: heart rate, respiration, muscle tone, skin color, and reflexes. Each factor is rated on a 3-point scale, from 0 = weakest to 3 = strongest. A low score indicates that the infant may have a problem.

thirty-five weeks, eight weeks after her birth. At this time, we were able to start following her with our assessment techniques. She still had respiratory problems and evidence of cerebral hemorrhage, which we suspected might have left her with mild neurological damage.

During this period her mother had visited her fifty-one times, her father forty-nine. When we asked them to join us as we assessed Clarissa, Mrs. D. was very happy, because she hoped we would find that, as she firmly believed, Clarissa "could do things for which no one seemed to credit her." She quickly added that she had seen a normal, full-term baby girl and realized how different she was from Clarissa. She knew it would take a long time, but the fact that the infant had survived and was already doing better made her feel that she would get stronger over time. Mrs. D. was back at work as an editor but planned to take time off when Clarissa came home. Both Clarissa's parents had formed a very intense relationship with the staff of the neonatal intensive care unit; the eagerness with which they cooperated bespoke their deep need for support.

As part of an ongoing study, we administered the Neonatal Behavioral Assessment Scale every two weeks from thirty-six to forty-four weeks of gestational age. Both mother and father took off time from work in order to be present on each occasion. The nurses had taught them how to administer necessary oxygen when Clarissa became too stressed, and they appeared to know when and how to handle her. But when she became stressed with our stimuli as we tested her, both parents would look discouraged and depressed. During the examination at thirty-six weeks, Clarissa became agitated, and as her color worsened, the exam had to be discontinued. However, the baby brought her right hand to her mouth and calmed herself. Mrs. D. noticed this and virtually beamed with delight. As Clarissa briefly watched the examiner's face to follow it, her mother could hardly contain herself. . . . Her parents seemed to be aware of all of her deficits but were able to pay attention to her attempts to control herself and other strengths. They tried to understand the limits of her responses—the narrow margin between her threshold for response and the level of stimuli above which she would be overwhelmed. . . .

At forty weeks of gestational age, Clarissa went home. She was still quite difficult to reach. She could console herself more easily than we could. The parents confirmed this, calling her a challenging baby, whom they just had to "wait to reach." On the next visit, Mrs. D. told the research team about their trouble with infertility and their determination to have a baby. Clarissa was a "special" child as a result. They were determined to see that Clarissa came along as well as possible now, "no matter what." The mother had maintained her breast milk for twelve weeks and was trying hard to feed Clarissa, despite all of these odds. . . . Her parents were bravely cheerful and found it difficult to admit that they had real worries about Clarissa's future. Though they reported the worries expressed by the neurologist about possible "brain damage," they usually just watched quietly as we examined their baby. . . .

The efforts of the research team gradually met with a little more success, and by forty-four weeks, Clarissa was less fragile, less easily overloaded, and a bit more reachable for auditory and visual responses. She still had to be very carefully swaddled and offered stimuli very quietly and slowly.

The parents watched us hungrily for cues as to how to handle her, and for encouragements. They talked uncomplainingly about the fact that they could never take her out, and watched her almost day and night. They met her frequent, uncontrollable crying periods with swaddling, frequent feedings, and all the techniques they had seen us apply. They used our visits as opportunities for support and reorganization for themselves, as well as for opportunities to watch for progress. The mother had decided to stay home with Clarissa indefinitely, and the father came home each night to relieve her. They supported each other through it all, each praising the other to us, but they also openly wished for an extended family which was nearby and could support them.

At the five-months visit, Clarissa's postural performance was worrisome enough that the research team decided to refer her to a nearby cerebral palsy intervention program for evaluation and treatment. In meetings with a psychiatrically trained social worker who was a member of our team, the parents voiced many questions regarding this referral and indicated their anger and frustration over the lack of definite answers to their questions about the child's long-term outcome.

Physical therapy was started at eight months. By nine months, Clarissa's ability to maintain an active playing period was increasing, and her responses to those around her were better. She no longer cried as intensely as at five months, but she was still difficult to regulate in her play and in sleep-wake transitions, and still needed to be fed at least every three hours day and night. She had also developed severely crossed eyes.

Her parents looked exhausted. After a long discussion of Clarissa's feeding and sleeping problems at nine months, the parents asked openly about her prematurity and the questions they had stored up about brain damage. "Would she ever completely recover?" This question had always been foremost on their minds, but they had not dared to admit it to each other, they said, until we "forced them to." It seemed a relief to be able to talk about it. They very quickly added that they were enjoying Clarissa and were aware of all the emerging skills that she showed. Indeed, on our assessments (the Bayley scale[2]), at nine months she was performing at her age, although the exam had required a low-keyed, patient approach on the part of the examiner, who was willing to spend twice as long as usual on her. . . .

On a return visit at eighteen months, we were impressed by the continued recovery in this child. She was still potentially disorganized, but she appeared to know her own capabilities and could defend herself from "falling apart." She now slept through the night and fed herself. She played by herself creatively. Her mother talked at some length about how difficult it had been to let Clarissa learn to play alone and to ignore her constant demands. At night, she had first let Clarissa cry for a while and then, to her surprise, Clarissa had begun to sleep through the

---

[2]Bayley scale: a scale indicating average milestones in development.

night. In the daytime, she had found that Clarissa could be independent and re-sourceful, if her initial whines were ignored. This was hard for Mrs. D., but she had been shown by the physiotherapist that Clarissa could be more outgoing and independent than she had realized. The child's vision had improved markedly with the aid of glasses. She spoke now in three- and four-word phrases, and her receptive language was entirely adequate.

When she was examined physically, she had an extended temper tantrum, which ended when her mother picked her up to comfort her. Tone and reflexes in her lower extremities were only slightly higher than normal, as was her sensitivity to auditory stimuli. She still walked with a slightly wide base. On the Bayley exam, she now performed somewhat above her age, with above-average scores on energy level and coordination of fine and gross motor skills.

Her parents described her as "fun, talking all the time, and rewarding." Indeed, she was delightful, determinedly stubborn, and charming in a social situation. When she had trouble with a task, she kept at it, repeating it over and over until she completed it. When she finally failed at a task, she quickly looked to her mother or father for support, as if failure could be very disappointing for her. We felt that her parents' determination to help this child recover was now reflected in her determination to succeed.

The parents were grateful for our care but felt that we had not "told them enough." Although they now had no real concern about her recovery, they would have liked to have been kept better appraised of each step in that recovery and what to expect. They seemed to feel that they had been struggling in a rather lonely way. But after this statement, they began to recount in detail their memories of each of our assessments and how much they'd learned from each one. While the physical examinations made the parents defensive, they enjoyed watching Clarissa perform on behavioral exams. They could see and feel that she'd learned from one time to another.

Response and Analysis

1. Clarissa's parents respond well to their daughter's unusual states, abilities, and deficits. Briefly describe a few examples of their interactions with Clarissa. How do you think the parents' skill in responding helps Clarissa overcome her precarious emotional and physical state? How did Clarissa's parents learn these skills?

2. Drs. Brazelton and Cramer state that Clarissa's parents felt that neither they nor the hospital staff had told them enough about potential problems or ways of handling Clarissa. Do you think the physicians knew what to expect? Should the hospital staff have told Clarissa's parents about every potential problem that might occur? Why or why not?

3. Medical services for a premature baby such as Clarissa are expensive. Who should pay for these services? Who should pay if the parents do not have insurance or if their insurance pays substantially less than the medical costs?

Research

Suppose you want to conduct a study to examine the development of fine motor skills among children born prematurely and those born full term. In your attempts to recruit participants, you have difficulty locating and recruiting boys to participate. In the premature birth group, you are able to recruit fourteen girls and four boys. In the full-term birth group, you are able to recruit sixteen girls and six boys. How might the differences in the number of boys and girls in your study influence your conclusions? What type of comparisons or conclusions will be most difficult to make?

THE FUSSY, HIGH-NEED BABY

William Sears and Martha Sears

Developmental Concepts
temperament, child's role in shaping parenting style,
development of empathy

William Sears, a pediatrician, and his wife, Martha Sears, a nurse, had a surprise when their fourth child, Hayden, was born. She was unlike their other children, and, had the Sears not felt successful raising their three sons, they might have worried more about their parenting skills. Hayden was full of energy; she was a demanding baby who fussed until her needs were met. Hoping to encourage self-regulation, Hayden's parents occasionally ignored her pleas but found this did not help. The Sears tell of sleepless nights and stressful days and of their strategies of loving and caring for Hayden. Their patience, discipline, and love paid off. Hayden, now in college and studying drama and psychology, is a secure, sensitive, and outgoing adult.

Sitting in the high school auditorium one spring evening, we proudly watched our seventeen-year-old daughter, Hayden, take her bows following the school's production of *Oklahoma!* She'd played the role of Ado Annie wonderfully, yet it was the Hayden we saw after the curtain call who warmed our hearts the most. We watched how she cared for her friends—the eye contact, the hugs, the delightfully natural social gestures, the expressivity that drew people, magnetlike, into her presence. As a tear or two flowed down her dad's cheeks, we thought back to "Hayden the handful"—the demanding baby, the strong-minded toddler, the challenging preschooler, the full-of-energy grade-schooler, and the exhausting teen. Now we are seeing a dynamic adult beginning to emerge. . . . Here's the story of the baby we got and the lessons we learned.

How She Acted

Hayden stretched us as parents and as individuals. Our first three children were relatively "easy" infants. They slept well and had a predictable feeding routine. Their needs were easy to identify—and satisfy. In fact, I began to suspect that parents in my pediatric practice who complained about their fussy babies were exaggerating. "What's all the fuss about difficult babies?" I wondered.

Then came Hayden, our fourth, whose birth changed our lives. Our first clue that she was going to be different came within a day or two. "I can't put her down" became Martha's recurrent theme. Breastfeeding for Hayden was not only a source of food, but a constant source of comfort. Martha became a human pacifier. Hayden would not accept substitutes. She was constantly in arms and at her mother's breast—and after a while those arms and breasts would get tired. Hayden's cries were not mere complaints, they were all-out alarms. Well-meaning friends suggested, "Just put her down and let her cry it out." That didn't work at all. Her extraordinary persistence kept her crying. Her cries did not fade away. They intensified if we didn't respond.

Hayden was very good at teaching us what she needed. "As long as we hold her, she's content" became our baby-care slogan. If we tried letting her fuss, she only fussed harder. We played "pass the baby." When Martha's arms gave out, into mine Hayden came. We used a front-pack carrier we had saved from brother Peter's baby days, but Hayden liked it only when we were out walking.

Nights were not bad in the early months, considering how intense she was by day. But around six months that all changed, and her nights became high-need. She rejected her crib as if it were a cage. After fourteen hours of baby holding, we longed for some nighttime relief. Hayden had other plans. As soon as we put her down in her crib and tried to creep out of the bedroom, she would awaken, howling in protest at having been left alone. Martha would nurse her back to sleep in the rocking chair, then put her back into her crib, and after an hour or less she would awaken again, demanding a repeat of the rocking-chair-and-nursing routine. It soon became evident that Hayden's need for human contact was as high at night as it was during the day.

How We Felt

If Hayden had been our first child, we would have concluded that it was our fault she couldn't settle herself, since we were inexperienced parents. But she was our fourth child, and by this time we felt we had a handle on caring for children. Nevertheless, Hayden did cause us to doubt our parenting abilities. Our confidence was getting shaky as our energy reserves were nearing empty. Our feelings about Hayden were as erratic as her behavior. Some days we were empathetic and nurturing; other days we were exhausted, confused, and resentful of her constant demands. Such mixed feelings were foreign to us, especially after parenting three easily managed babies. Soon it became obvious that Hayden was a different kind of baby. She was wired differently from other babies.

The challenge for us was to figure out how to mother and father this unique little person while also conserving enough energy for our other three children—and ourselves.

Hayden Opened Us Up as Persons

Instead of defensively getting caught up in the fear of spoiling, we started listening to what Hayden had been trying to tell us from the moment she exited the womb. As soon as we discarded our preconceived ideas of how babies are supposed to be and accepted the reality of how Hayden was, we all got along much better.

If she fussed when we put her down but was content when we held her, we would hold her. If she needed to nurse a lot, Martha would nurse her. We believed Hayden knew what she needed, and fortunately she had the persistence to keep telling us until we understood.

Hayden taught us that tiny babies don't manipulate, they communicate. A child psychologist friend who was visiting us was interested in Hayden's cry. She was impressed that the cry was not an angry, demanding one but rather an expectant one, as if Hayden knew she would be heard.

Hayden caused us to reevaluate our job description as parents. We had always thought an effective parent needed to be in constant control. Then we realized that mind-set was self-defeating. It assumes that there is an adversarial relationship between parent and child: The baby is "out to get you," so you better get her first. Hayden made us realize our role was not to control her. It was to *manage* her, and to help her learn to control herself.

What helped us get over the fear-of-spoiling and the fear-of-being-manipulated mind-set was the realization that it was better to err on the side of being overreactive and overresponsive. As we worked on developing a balance of appropriate responses, there were times when we responded too slowly and times when we jumped too quickly, but we felt that when in doubt, it was better to be responsive. Children who are perhaps indulged a bit (as many firstborn high-need children are) will at least develop a healthy self-image and trust in their parents. With this foundation it is easier to back off a bit as you try to create a healthy balance between parents' needs and child's. The child of parents who respond too little develops a poor self-image, and a distance develops between parent and child. This situation is harder to remedy. I have never heard parents in my pediatric practice say that they wish they hadn't held their baby so much. In fact, most, if able to rewind their parenting tape, would hold their baby more.

We also considered one of the earliest teachings that Martha had learned as a nurse and I had learned as a physician: First, do no harm (*primum non nocere*). We decided that if we tried to squelch Hayden's personality, we would be doing her harm and crippling her development. Our job as parents was not to change Hayden into a behavioral clone of every other baby. It would have been wrong to try to change her. (How dull the world would be if all babies acted the same!) It was better to widen our expectations and accept her the way she was, not the way we wished she was. Our parental role was like that of a gardener: We couldn't change the color of the flower or the day when it would bloom, but we could pull the weeds and prune the plant so it blossomed more beautifully. Our role was to channel Hayden's behavior and nurture her special qualities so that instead of being a liability, these temperament traits would later work to her advantage and serve her well. . . .

Sleep, or rather the lack of it, became a major problem. Actually, for the first six months Hayden slept quite well, waking once or twice at night to be fed. She slept in a cradle right next to our bed, and when she stirred, Martha would nudge the cradle into motion or pat her. Unless she was hungry, she'd settle right back to sleep. Then Hayden learned to sit up, and the cradle was no longer safe. We replaced it with a crib up against the wall about twelve feet from our bed. Somehow she knew that was too far away, or maybe it was that the crib couldn't be nudged to rock. She woke more and more, until one night she was awake every hour. Martha said, "I don't care what the books say, I've got to get some sleep." Where upon she nestled Hayden next to her in our bed. Once we discarded the picture of a self-soothing baby sleeping solo in a crib, we slept together happily. . . .

Early on we realized that learning to live with Hayden meant channeling her unique personality traits to work not only to her advantage but also to our advantage. Her keen awareness made her more sensitive to our moods, so we learned that when Hayden was being childish we had to be "adultish." Hayden taught us the concept of mirroring: Children, especially hypersensitive ones, easily pick up their parents' moods. If a tantrum was about to erupt and we reflected an "it's okay, no problem" attitude, she would often mirror our peace and settle down. If we let ourselves get angry or worried about the tantrum, our anxiety just added fuel to her fire. When Hayden protested our instructions and flew into a rage, we needed to stay calm. When she lost her self-control, we had to hang on to ours. If we lost our composure—and many times we did—it took twice as long for her to settle down. Acting like the adult in charge set a calmer mood that helped put a crumbling child back together. . . .

As Hayden grew, her neediness remained but her personality blossomed. One of the earliest qualities we noticed was her sensitivity, her ability to care and comfort when playmates were hurt or upset. As a preschooler, she had already developed a keen sense of justice and social values. Often she would say "That's not right" or "How sad." Her love of people and her ability to connect with them was another payoff we witnessed. She would be aware of other children who needed mothering, and she would do what she could to help. Her sense of intimacy was appropriate, giving eye contact or a touch on the arm during a conversation. She had a confident way of being in the presence of adults. A child psychiatrist who was at our home one evening remarked, "Hayden knows where her body is in space." We knew what that meant. Because she had been held and nursed and responded to appropriately, Hayden already had a good sense of herself as a unique physical presence and she responded to others in their uniqueness. She was able even then to affirm each person she met. Since Hayden was used to being understood and responded to, she could express herself comfortably. . . . It's no wonder that through her grade school and high school years, she enjoyed and excelled at being onstage. Her chosen course of study in college, if you haven't already guessed, is psychology and drama.

Response and Analysis

1. William and Martha Sears describe their daughter Hayden as temperamentally very different from her siblings. What is temperament, and what produces it? If you have siblings, how do their temperaments differ from those of each other and from yours? (If you don't have siblings, think of siblings in families you know.) Which of those differences do you believe were present at birth? Which developed after birth?

2. Parents shape their children's behavior, but children also shape their parents' behavior. How does Hayden shape her parents' behavior? How might a child's temperament interact with the parents' personalities and needs to affect the attachment process? Discipline styles?

3. Hayden's parents describe her as concerned about others and responsive to their needs. To what extent do you think that Hayden's parents helped her to develop empathy? In what ways can parents develop empathy in their children?

Research

Developmental psychologists use a variety of methodological approaches. Suppose you are interested in using the case study method to examine how parents respond to a fussy or high-need baby during the baby's first two years. What are two advantages and two disadvantages of the case-study approach? What types of questions cannot be answered using this approach? Assume that you have scheduled an appointment to interview the mother and father. Make a list of topics that you would discuss with them.

PERPETUAL MOTION:
A CURIOUS BABY

Anne Lamott

Developmental Concepts
gross motor development, sensorimotor period, object
permanence, autonomy

Author Anne Lamott draws on her spirited sense of humor to tell about her baby, Sam, during the second half of his first year of life. Sam is on the move. Activity is essential to his development, and he shows increasing control over gross and fine motor skills. Like most infants in their first year, Sam tries various techniques of crawling until he is able to move about. As he learns to crawl and then to stand, Sam discovers new talents. Holding onto the couch, he can move his body and dance. Standing by the coffee table, he can create a flat plane by picking up and then flinging items off, one by one. He lives in the here and now. Will Sam search for an object that disappears from sight? Does he understand that a hidden object continues to exist? How do Sam's developing cognitive skills change his life?

February 23

[At six months] Sam can sit up by himself . . . without having to be propped up with pillows. I used to surround him entirely with pillows so he could sit around without my having to hold him. Donna[1] used to call it Fort Samuel, and she used to tell him that Fort Samuel was a state of mind. But now he can sit up by himself. Everything is going by so quickly. You know how when you're at the library, and you get one of those reels of tape that hold two weeks' worth of newspapers, and you put the reel on and then wind it forward really fast to the date you're looking for, but you see every day pass by for about half a minute? That's what it feels like to me now.

   Sam, who was so recently larval and incompetent, is almost crawling. He moved backwards half a foot tonight. I feel that these are his first steps out of the present. He used to trip out only on whatever was within his narrow vision and grasp, but now he sees something a few feet away and he gets this glinty . . . look in his eyes, like in the old cartoons where someone gets a greedy brainstorm, blinks, and we hear the sound of a cash register and see the dollar signs in his eyes.

---
[1]Donna: a friend of Anne Lamott.

He's crawling inexorably away from the now. He's crawling toward anticipated pleasures. Soon there will be scheming and manipulation, a dedication to certain outcomes, to attaining certain things and storing them for later. I'm trying so hard to learn to live in the now, to bring my mind back to the present, while Sam is learning to anticipate and plan, to want things that are far away.

March 24

He moves so fast these days, like a lizard. He's babbling with great incoherent animation. He gets on all fours and rocks, like he's about to take off, like Edwin Moses in the starting block. His new thing is that he likes to stick his fingers in your mouth and examine your teeth. He does it every time we nurse. Maybe he wants to be a periodontist when he grows up. It's a little disconcerting. He'll stare at my mouth for a minute when he's lying in my arms, and then reach in with these tiny monkey fingers and go tooth by tooth, checking each one for problems. . . .

March 28

One thing about Sam, one thing about having a baby, is that each step of the way you simply cannot imagine loving him any more than you already do, because you are bursting with love, loving as much as you are humanly capable of—and then you do, you love him even more.

He's figuring out little concepts all the time these days, like that if something falls out of his hands, it is not instantly vaporized but just might be found somewhere on the floor. Even a week ago Sam was like some rich guy who drops some change and doesn't even give it a second glance, but now when he drops something, he slowly cranes his neck and peers downward, as if the thing fell to the floor of a canyon.

March 29

Today is his seven-month birthday. . . . He's a crawling guy now. He crawls in this lumbering, barrel-chested way, like a Komodo dragon. I saw glee and smugness and danger in his face today, as if he had just been handed the keys to the car.

March 31

He's been sitting up by himself for a long time now, no longer needing to be surrounded by pillows, but I can see that he remains Fort Samuel, because as Donna keeps reminding me, Fort Samuel is simply a state of mind. Also, I finally set up the playpen the people from my church gave me. At first I thought we'd started it too late, because he'd only last a few minutes before he'd look completely bereft and forsaken and dying, like when the Bushman in *The Gods Must Be Crazy* was in that jail cell. If I didn't pick him up right away, he'd start to cry. But we have had playpen practice for a little while twice a day, and today he sat in it for twenty minutes, playing with his toys and babbling.

April 3

Uncle Steve came by just in time for playpen practice, which Steve immediately dubbed Office Hours. "Time for your office hours, honey," he said, popping him into the playpen, and Sam entertained himself with his toys for quite a while, throwing things, banging toys together, putting smaller toys inside of bigger ones. I simply could not believe my eyes. Comparing this to even a month ago, let alone six, when he couldn't do anything but nurse and poop, when he couldn't hold his head up, focus, or chew, I felt like this was a miraculous apparition, one I would hold up against Bernadette seeing the Virgin in the grotto near Lourdes. . . .

May 20

Sam can climb stairs now. . . . Today at church he played with the kids in the back room for the first time. He was in his walker, and these little kids are possibly the most stunningly gorgeous people on earth. They adore him, and they push him hard in his walker from one person to the next, all the way across the room. . . . All the little kids including Sam roar with laughter, like they're all in love.

May 31

I don't remember who said this, but there really are places in the heart you don't even know exist until you love a child. Sam's been teaching me how to play again, at my ripe old age. His favorite thing right now is for me to hide a Cheerio in my mouth and then to let it peek out a tiny bit, and he goes in after it with this great frantic concentration, like it's a diamond. . . .

June 16

This memory thing is really interesting. Before, every time Sam went into a room—the bathroom, for instance—he would be almost beside himself with wonder and amazement, like it was his first trip to FAO Schwarz.[2] Now he recognizes it. It's not quite old-hat yet, but he sees the bathtub and he remembers that he loves it and he tries to thrust and squirm his way over to it. It's funny that he loves the bathtub so much. He didn't always. But mostly he loves to toss stuff into the tub when it's empty, and then he loves to gaze endlessly down into it, with wonder, like it's a garden in full bloom.

---

[2]FAO Schwarz: a toy store.

He's heavily into flinging things. He dismantles everything he can get his hands on, pulling every possible book and chotchke off every possible table and shelf and flinging them over his shoulder. . . .

He almost never actually *takes* anything and crawls away with it, but he'll get to the coffee table and systematically, often without any expression, lift and then drop or fling every single magazine, book, cup, or whatever to the ground. His grim expression suggests he's got a lot to do and just really doesn't want to be bothered until he's done. . . .

June 21

This boy can dance, Mama; he still can't walk, but he pulls himself into a standing position, holds on to the couch or chair or leg or whatever is nearby, and begins to bounce and gyrate. This boy can rock and roll. It's such a miracle. It seems that only yesterday he was so pupal, and now he's Michael Jackson. . . .

He can wave now, baby-style, hinging his fingers up and down over his palm. It's really more than either Pammy or I can handle. What next? I asked her. Juggling? Calligraphy?

He eats almost anything now. He took a nice fat ripe plum today and plowed into it like a gorilla, with buckets of juice and saliva pouring forth everywhere. Then he let the red skin emerge slowly from his mouth, like a rejected dollar bill from a change machine.

Response and Analysis

1. According to Anne Lamott, at what age did Sam learn to sit up by himself? Crawl? At what ages do most children attain these skills? What other physical abilities does she say Sam developed in his first seven months?

2. Lamott says that when her son used to drop something, he never looked for it. Now he "cranes his neck and peers downward, as if the thing fell to the floor of a canyon." According to Piaget, what cognitive ability is Sam demonstrating? When do children typically attain this ability? How have the findings of recent research modified Piaget's theory about this ability?

3. When her son first learned to crawl, Lamott saw "glee and smugness and danger" in his face. Nearly three months later, she describes how he removed, dropped, or threw every item from the coffee table. What purpose might these actions serve? What emotional states does Lamott attribute to her child as he performs these actions? Which emotions are first evident in children and which develop later?

4. In describing Sam's use of the playpen, Lamott writes that she's giving him "playpen practice." What do you think are the benefits and drawbacks of allowing a child to play in a playpen?

Research

Suppose you are interested in studying the relationship between children's play—alone or with others—and their health. You would like to observe children between the ages of one and two years at a daycare facility.

Research involving human participants is governed by a variety of ethical principles, so before conducting a study you must secure approval from the human participants Institutional Review Board at your college or university. The review board is designed to ensure that your procedures are ethical and protect the rights and dignity of the participants. To conduct the study, you need to obtain permission from the daycare facility as well as detailed health reports from each child's pediatrician. You also need to obtain the parents' informed consent for their child's participation and to maintain confidentiality of records and other information. Why are informed consent and confidentiality important? What information would you need to keep confidential? Why?

section 2

EARLY CHILDHOOD

"Does a mouse know it's a mouse?" Roger
asked me when he was five.
"What do you mean?" I asked.
"Well, like I know I'm me.*"*
I was caged. "Tell me what you think,"
I said.
"Well, I think a mouse doesn't know it's a
mouse, but I don't know why I know
that."

SELMA H. FRAIBERG, *The Magic Years*

Children between the ages of two years and six years love exploration and have a tremendous appetite for learning. When they play a game of tag, they not only have fun but also stimulate their brains and develop motor skills. Playing a game of house or doctor and taking turns assuming the roles of parent, child, patient, doctor, or nurse can help children become familiar with how adults manage family relations or how health-care professionals provide for the sick. Play can also help reinforce family roles or expectations and make children less fearful when they themselves are ill. In short, play becomes a way of making complex real-life situations more manageable.

During early childhood, preschoolers begin to recognize the rudiments of time and distance. Their language and cognitive skills increase dramatically, which allow their social relationships to become more complex. Preschoolers face increasing demands to become socialized members of the culture. They must learn to restrain themselves in some ways and exert themselves in others. Children gradually master social skills and self-control, which accelerates their sense of autonomy and initiative, but young children require regular reassurance and support. Preschoolers express their emotions in posture, movement, and speech, and much of their charm comes from the way they so easily reveal their struggles and triumphs.

Madeleine—who was introduced in Section 1 during her first two years of life—is now in her third year. She is beginning to understand gender, but does not yet realize that one's gender is permanent. Like all children, Madeleine watches and gathers clues that help her recognize the important differences between males and females. By playing make-believe games and using language, Madeleine has also begun to think of situations and possibilities beyond her immediate experiences. Some of those are imaginary and frightening, while others are profound: How was she different in the past? How was the world different in the past? Where did everything come from? Madeleine's questions show that she has begun to think about herself as a being with a past and a future.

Vivian Gussin Paley, a nursery school teacher, takes us into her classroom to observe her students at play. Mollie and her friends use play and language to represent hopes and fears. They create imaginary situations and take on roles that change easily—a ballerina, the ballet itself, a lion, a statue, a defender with a gun. For Mollie and her classmates, pretend play and creative play are ways to represent and act out what they know, to expand their knowledge, and to establish true friendships outside their families.

Harry Crews recalls becoming aware of himself as a conscious being in the world when he was four years old. By this age, most children also begin to develop a pattern of sequential event memories, and, although those memories might not always be entirely accurate, they begin to define one's personal history and sense of self. Their play has become complex, often expressing an understanding of adult relationships. Crews and his friends construct elaborate imaginary lives for the models in a Sears catalog, and their stories reveal much about their world.

Some children, particularly those in poverty or under other stresses (such as abuse), often don't have the luxury of long periods of imaginative play. Frank McCourt grew up in a family that faced extreme poverty, and before he was five years old he and his family suffered the losses of three children. As the oldest child, McCourt was sometimes needed to help find food or fuel, or to care for his siblings. He describes his experiences and the great emotional burdens he carried, and he conveys how children in harsh circumstances may begin to develop empathy. McCourt's memoir is a reminder that great numbers of children are forced to cope daily with poverty, which puts them at greater risk of malnourishment, illness, delays in cognitive, language, and social development, and even death.

Annie Dillard tells about a time when as a young child she used reasoning to cope with fantasy-based fears. She saw strange shadows moving across her bedroom wall at night, and these triggered fears of a mysterious creature in her bedroom. However, at five years old, Dillard was capable of reasoning in a way that most three- and four-year-olds are not. As Dillard gradually connected the shadows with harmless events outside her room, her childhood egocentrism gave way to more mature reasoning. It is fascinating to read how she tried to master the situation by shifting between her rational explanation and her scary fantasies.

As children move through early childhood toward middle childhood, reasoning and self-regulation become increasingly important. For children diagnosed with attention-deficit/hyperactivity disorder (ADHD), self-control is difficult. Because the disorder is often (but not always) accompanied by disruptive behavior, it can create considerable problems for children, their families, daycare centers, and schools. Ann Colin's son, Willie, was diagnosed with ADHD. Like approximately one-third of children with ADHD, he did not respond positively to medication. Fortunately, he responded to cognitive therapy and learned to modify some of his impulsive behaviors.

MADELEINE'S UNDERSTANDING OF GENDER AND TIME

Brian Hall

Developmental Concepts
gender identity, preoperational thought, understanding time

Two-year-old Madeleine is pondering big issues: How are boys and girls similar and different? Will she grow up to be a man or a woman? Where does the world come from? Madeleine knows that she is a girl and appears to understand that girls grow into women and boys grow into men. Her father is taken aback, however, when Madeleine proclaims that she will lift heavy objects when she grows up to be a man! Her sense of gender constancy—the understanding that gender does not change—has not yet developed. Indeed, the understanding that one's gender is permanent does not typically appear until ages four to five years.

As Madeleine's language skills continue to develop, Hall is curious about her understanding of time. For Madeleine, an event that happened just five minutes ago occurred "last night"; they had breakfast "last night"! She has not yet developed skills for placing memories of events along anything but the most basic time continuum (for example, a long time ago, last night, now, later, "when I'm big"). Soon she will understand, and soon she will be three years old!

[At the store] Madeleine had been holding up her two index fingers and beaming "I'm two!" and the charmed cashier had been laughing and chirping "She's so cute" when Madeleine decided to change the subject and sang out, "Daddy has a penis!" The cashier continued to smile, saying nothing. Either she assumed she had misheard or she was quietly memorizing my face. I paid and left.

It had been some months since Madeleine had learned the words "boy," "girl," "man," and "woman," and now she was in the process of tackling the next level of classification: male and female. . . .

She seemed to understand my explanation that boys grew into men and girls grew into women, and that what distinguished the sexes was the possession of a penis or a vagina. . . .

My confidence that she understood gender was rattled as she began saying, whenever she needed me to lift something heavy for her, "When I a big man [I'll be able to do it]!" This seemed to be her only instance of confusion, however, and I wondered if the word "big" was throwing her off. "Big," she well knew from our daily exclamations, was what she was getting, but as an epithet she often heard it yoked with "man" (on the theme of Daddy-as-giant) and never with "woman." (As it happened, none of our female friends or relatives were large.) "Big man" might have been a syntactical unit to her, bigman, the thing that bigkids of either gender grew into.

In any case, the phrase "when I a big man" did clearly suggest another dawning awareness: that of change. One day she would be able to carry the milk jug to the table. One day she would be allowed to use the sharp knife. The future! This was the first indication that she had some conscious image of it beyond the next few hours.

For me, the most intriguing mystery about Madeleine was her sense of time. She said "last night" when referring to things she remembered, and "tomorrow" when referring to things she expected, so she did have some sense of time stretching in two different directions away from her, but the relative distances were vague. "Last night," on rare occasions, meant last night, but usually it meant five minutes or an hour ago. "A long time ago" had initially been reserved for the twin cornerstones of her consciousness, laid when time began: the chicken that bit her foot ("Pecked!") and the two dogs that jumped up ("One!"). But now she also used the phrase to indicate things that had happened one or more days previously, apparently having decided that "last night" didn't stretch back that far: "A long time ago, I said, 'Aahh! I don't want my diapers on!'"

Actually, yesterday. The original "aahh!" had been prolonged and earsplitting, while this knowing reference to it was brief and earsplitting. Madeleine began frequently to refer back to crying episodes, and the time lag shortened to a few minutes. She had discovered that she could use time and memory to step away from her emotions and examine them. She called up her previous self—screaming her head off, unable to listen to any appeal—and standing next to this inconsolable dervish, became her interpreter, her liaison to the world of adult reason. "Why I crying?" she would ask with genuine curiosity, and I might say, "You didn't want to leave Katha's house." "Why we go?" "We had to go because . . ." Her mood during these posttrauma sessions was always one of intense relief, as the storm was taken out of the hands of malignant and unfathomable gods and shown to be the natural consequence of two colliding fronts: her understandable desire, my reasonable inability to satisfy said desire.

She began to take the same approach to happy moments. In the first instance I remember, I was holding her in one arm while breaking ice on the kitchen counter with a heavy metal spoon. The ice sometimes shot off the counter and streaked away across the floor, and the sight of this inanimate object being disobedient, running away like a girl whose diapers needed changing, made Madeleine shout with laughter. A minute later she informed me, "I yaff! 'Ha ha ha!'" and the tinkling, jokey sound of her imitation laughter made me laugh as well. The technique allowed her not only to view her amusement from outside (why had she laughed?) but also to extend it a little into the long, flat stretches of non-laughter, non-ice-breaking, that her developing sense of time enabled her to glimpse all around the isolated, ecstatic peaks of her life. Here were the beginnings of both self-consciousness (she was a girl who laughed) and nostalgia (remember when we broke ice and laughed?). Here were two more layers, like refractive filters, over her perceptions; two more steps toward sophistication, away from freshness. . . .

A long time ago, she was a little baby. She looked at old pictures of herself and handled old clothes that she remembered wearing but that were now too small. We measured her against the door frame, and two months later did it again, and she was more than an inch taller. "Look how big I'm are!"

A long time ago, Wolf licked her in the face and she cried. She didn't remember that, but she remembered looking at the photographs of it.

A long time ago, she had no hair. Now she twirled it until a knot came off on her finger, and she handed it to me, laughing, "That's not hair. That's fuzz!" (I had asked the grandmothers if any of my or Pamela's siblings had ever twirled their hair, and they had said no, none.)

A long time ago, a chicken bit her foot.

A long time ago, two dogs jumped up on her.

Last night Ti-ti hit her, and she cried "Aahh!" Why did Ti-ti hit her?

A long time ago, she rode a bus and a man gave her John the Rhino.

A long time ago, she rode the merry-go-round.

Last night we ate the Chinese buffet.

Last night we had breakfast.

A long time ago, we measured her against the door frame.

Now she would hold up one of her shoes and ask me where it came from. "From Woolworth's," I would say. "And before that"—I would look at the label—"from China." And her sock? "Since it's cotton, perhaps from the Carolinas." We would find China and the Carolinas on our globe. Places where the past dwelled.

Inevitably, one day she would ask, "Where Maya from?"

In other words, what had happened before the chicken pecked her foot? Going backward, how small did she get? Why, since she could remember the chicken, the dogs, the merry-go-round, the buffet, why couldn't she remember anything before the chicken?

"You came from Mama's tummy," I said. I couldn't discern anything in her face. What did she understand? That all of our pretend Madeleine-eating referred back to a real swallowing of her?

Not understanding it myself, I had unthinkingly coughed up the clichéd response, but it wasn't the answer to her question. . . .

And as though I had answered that question, Madeleine went on. She threw out her arms and asked, "Where all this from?" She said it, I thought, with a tinge of exasperation. What unreasonable place was this that demanded such a question?

"Do you mean the house? The world?"

"The world."

I had a load of diapers to wash, so I only said, "That's a big question." . . .

By the middle of March she had learned the months and the milestones in each that were steps toward the blessed day. At the end of March came Pamela's birthday. At the beginning of April was Easter. Then came May Day. By mid-May we would have tulips. And toward the end of May was the Memorial Day weekend ("Here," I pointed), and on the Friday before that weekend was—ding ding ding!— the opening of the park merry-go-round.

Once she had that nailed down, we could venture further. After May came June, toward the end of which Conor or Cora[2] would be born. In July was America's birthday. In August was my birthday. And in September, Madeleine would turn . . . ?

"Three!"

Exactly.

From counting seconds to counting years, we were laying down the rudiments of the grid, the net, with which Madeleine could catch time. One day (she could see it right on the calendar), she would be three years old. . . .

Unimaginable, really. Out there somewhere hung the merry-go-round, and spring, and adulthood.

Response and Analysis

1. What has Madeleine learned about gender? What misunderstandings does she have? Are her views about gender and gender assignment typical of children her age? Why or why not?

2. At age two, Madeleine has begun to reflect on her own behavior and experiences, as evidenced by comments such as "I yaff!" and "Why I crying?" What might these self-reflective comments reveal about her cogni-tive development, including the development of a sense of self?

3. Brian Hall suggests that Madeleine's phrase, "when I a big man" may reveal clues about her understanding of time and gender. What is Madeleine's understanding of time? How might a preschooler's comments about the past and the future reflect the development of memory skills?

4. Suppose you volunteer to work at a preschool where a teacher asks you to develop

---

[2]Conor or Cora: names for Madeleine's future sibling.

a lesson to help the children learn about their family history (for example, grandparents, parents, and siblings). How would your knowledge about preschoolers' understanding of gender and time influence the lessons and activities you include in the program? Give a short description of one activity that you might design.

Research

Suppose you want to conduct a study to examine children's understanding of time. Your participants are boys and girls between the ages of four and eight. You measure understanding of time by having each child arrange sets of pictures into simple sequences that have a beginning, a middle, and an end. For example, one picture might show an inflated balloon, a second might show an uninflated balloon, and a third might show someone blowing up a balloon. For each set of pictures that the children arrange, you score the sequence as follows: 0 (illogical sequence), 1 (partially logical sequence), or 2 (logical sequence). Is this a reliable way to assess children's understanding of time? A valid way? Would you show the same pictures to all children regardless of their age? Why or why not? If not, what would you do? Briefly discuss one other way that you might use to assess children's understanding of time.

MOLLIE IN PRESCHOOL

Vivian Gussin Paley

Developmental Concepts
pretend play, preoperational period, peer
relationships, symbolic thinking

Vivian Gussin Paley, a talented teacher at the University of Chicago's nursery school, brings us into her classroom to observe the interactions among Mollie and her classmates. Paley uses a tape recorder to keep track of the children's interactions and conversations, and her rich stories convey the children's cognitive, social, and physical capabilities.

Mollie and her classmates are engaged in pretend play and are creating make-believe and imaginary situations. Their play is intrinsically motivated and creative, and it follows rules they make up and agree to. Mollie and her friends set up "scary" situations. When those in one group pretend to be monsters or witches, the children in another group try various means of defense, such as hiding in a play house or holding pretend guns. Mollie is especially creative in finding a defense. When another child says that a monster is on the way and offers Mollie a gun, she refuses it. "I'm a statue," Mollie announces. Note how the children use toys to interact, how they develop friendships in their play, and how they explore gender roles. These delightful, inventive children are, as Paley says, involved in "experimental theater."

Learning is a reciprocal process; Mollie is as much teacher as student. She tells Christopher that he, like Peter Rabbit, will have blackberries and milk if he is good, and warns Margaret not to dial the fire department because Curious George "false alarmed them." She urges Erik to plant the seeds he finds in the playground so he can climb up the beanstalk "when the giant is not there," and asks Emily to help her build a brick house "so the wolf doesn't huff us." . . .

Mollie . . . knows how to bring book characters into conversation, play, and stories, and the new stories she creates out of old ones produce an exciting sense of continuity.

Today, for example, she puts "Mushroom in the Rain," "The Three Pigs," and "Hansel and Gretel" into a Wonderwoman story. In the original "Mushroom in the Rain," a butterfly, a mouse, and a sparrow are drenched in a heavy downpour, then sheltered under a mushroom by a kindly ant. A frightened rabbit and a hungry fox also enter the story, but Mollie gives star billing to the wet butterfly.

"I want to be the wet butterfly and Wonderwoman. First he goes under the mushroom. Now we got to do the big, bad wolf and the three pigs and the fox is going to catch the butterfly and put it in the cage, that one from Hansel. Then Wonderwoman comes. Then I open the cage and the wet butterfly goes under the mushroom because the ant says to come in."

How has Mollie learned to integrate these bits and pieces into a sensible whole? No one else offers Christopher blackberries and milk if he is good or unites the big, bad wolf with a fox to make trouble for a butterfly. However, it is the sort of storytelling that is heard every day during play: Cinderella and Darth Vader put the baby to bed while Superman serves tea and saves the baby from the witch just as Daddy comes home from work and sits down to eat a birthday cake.

If Mollie is quicker than most to transfer the process into her stories it is because, more than most children, she sees life as a unified whole. To her, fantasy characters and real people all communicate in the same language. . . .

It is especially easy to witness in the doll corner, where family matters dominate. Samantha and Amelia are there now, covered with veils and shawls, chanting, "We're getting married." Libby enters, frowning; she senses she is being left out of an important ceremony.

"What are you doing, Samantha?"

"Watch out, Libby. We're getting married."

"Can I get married with you?"

"Hurry up, Amelia. Put on the lace, honey."

"Just us, Libby."

"I'm getting married too," Libby says. "By myself."

"Not with us, Libby, 'cause you didn't see my flower girl dress and only Amelia saw it."

"I saw my own flower girl dress and *I'm* going to the ballet."

"So am I," Samantha counters.

"I'm going to *be* the ballet."

"Well, I know how to dance and you don't."

"Yes I do!" Libby begins to cry. "Teacher, Samantha says I can't dance."

"I'm sure you can, Libby."

"She's stupid! She's a liar."

Mollie has been watching the scene from the telephone table. She walks over to the two angry girls and smiles. "Guess what! Margaret's coming to my house today. She's my friend."

Her declaration is not out of context. The argument she interrupts is not about marriage or the ballet, but concerns who is playing with whom. This is the proper time to announce that she will play with Margaret, all by herself, at her house today.

The girls look at Mollie and Margaret and remember that they too are friends. Samantha dials the telephone. "Hello, Libby? Call the police. There's a noise. I think it's a lion."

"Yeah. I hear roaring. Turn off the light. Pretend we're not home."

Margaret takes Mollie's hand as they leave. Neither one is comfortable in the doll corner when the lion is at the door.

A few minutes later Mollie returns, uncertainly. She knows the girls are only pretending something bad is about to happen; but what if the bad thing doesn't know it's pretend? Nonetheless, Mollie decides to stay, keeping one foot outside the drama.

"Go to sleep, Mollie," Libby orders. "There might be something dangerous. You won't like it."

"I know it," Mollie says. "But I got a bunk bed at home and I sleep there."

"Bunk beds are too scary," Amelia says.

"Why are they?" Mollie looks worried.

"It's a monster, Mollie. Hide!"

"I know. But there's no monsters in my house today."

"You have to hide, Mollie. It's a real monster."

"I'm going to hide by the teacher."

"No, Mollie, stay here. Under here. Under the cover."

"I'm going to be a statue," Mollie whispers. "So he won't see me."

"He won't get me," Libby says, "because I've got a real gun. You want one?"

Mollie shakes her head. "I'm a statue."

"No, Mollie, hide. Come here. I'll hide you. The boys are going to scare us." Libby looks around for an available boy and catches sight of Fredrick at the painting table. "Watch out!" she shouts. "Fredrick is coming! He's a monster! Hide!"

Fredrick drops his brushes and rushes into the doll corner on all fours. "Roar!" He arches his back and claws the air. "G-r-r!"

"Teacher! Fredrick's scaring Mollie!"

"I'm a lion. I'm roaring."

"Is he scaring you, Mollie?"

"No."

"Is anyone scaring you?"

"The bunk bed," she answers solemnly. . . .

My games consistently miss the point of *their* games: the recognition and repetition of what is obvious to all. The [three-year-olds] have been demonstrating these facts to me for months, but I keep adding complications. A few days later the unadorned simplicity of it all comes across to me.

We are playing an invention of mine called "Who's missing, who's missing, guess who's not here," in which one child hides behind a screen while another child tries to guess his identity. The fours play the game easily, giving appropriate hints and not peeking. I cannot, however, convince the threes to observe two important rules: do not reveal the hidden person's name and, if you are the one who is hiding, do not come out before your name is guessed.

Suddenly I see the game through younger eyes. "Let's play a different way," I tell the children. "We'll all watch the hider, we'll pretend we don't know who it is, and then we'll all say who it is."

We sing the original refrain, changing the last line to suit the new rules: "Who's missing, who's missing, guess who's not here. It's Mollie, it's Mollie, now she is here."

Together we watch Mollie hide and after a moment of closing our eyes we call out her name. Mollie jumps out laughing. "It's me!"

The new game is a splendid success, not unlike the three-year-olds' hide-and-seek, in which they pretend to hide and pretend to seek. Carrie has her own version: she hides a favorite possession, then asks a teacher to help her find it. She pretends to look for it as she takes the teacher directly to the missing item. "Oh, here's my dolly's brush!" she squeals delightedly. All these games resist the unknown and the possibility of loss. They are designed to give the child control in the most direct way.

Sometimes, however, the child has no control; something is really missing. Then the threes are likely to approach the problem as if the question is "What is *not* missing? This is exactly what happens when I try to direct the children's attention to an empty space in the playground. Over the weekend, an unsafe climbing structure has been removed. The doll corner window overlooks the area that housed the rickety old frame.

"See if you can tell what's missing from our playground?" I ask.

"The sandbox."

"The squirrely tree."

"The slide."

"But I can *see* all those things. They're still in the playground. Something else was there, something very big, and now it's gone."

"The boat."

"Mollie, look. There's the boat. I'm talking about a big, brown, wooden thing that was right there where my finger is pointing."

"Because there's too much dirt."

"But what was on top of the place where there's too much dirt?"

"It could be grass. You could plant grass."

Libby and Samantha see us crowded around the window and walk over to investigate. "Where's the climbing house?" Libby asks. "Someone stole the climbing house."

"No one stole the house, Libby. We asked some men to take it down for us. Remember how shaky it was? We were afraid somebody would fall."

The threes continue staring, confused. I should have anticipated their response and urged that the structure be dismantled during school hours. After all, these are the children who scrub a clean table because it had playdough on it the day before, and worry about birds coming in to bother the blocks.

"Does everyone remember the climbing house? Here, I'll draw a picture. Let's see, it went up this high and here were some steps. . . ."

"Where are the steps?" Mollie asks.

"The men chopped everything up and took it all away in a truck."

"Where are they stepping to?"

"The steps are not steps any more. I'll bet they're using all the old wood for firewood."

"They use them to step out of the fire," Mollie says. . . .

[And so] the children [are able to] avoid the disturbing image of a missing stairway. . . .

Response and Analysis

1. What rules do Mollie and her schoolmates follow when playing hide-and-seek? Why do the children not hide out of sight when playing the game? How do they react when something is missing? Why is a sense of control important for preschool children?

2. What cognitive abilities do you see in Mollie and her friends that represent Piaget's preoperational period? Briefly describe two examples of assimilation or accommodation that Mollie and her friends display.

3. Mollie and her friends create stories that involve magical, imaginative thinking and the acting out of roles. How might this form of sociodramatic play help children learn about social roles? How might such play help them learn about and manage their emotions or personal concerns?

4. Suppose that you volunteer to be a teacher's aide at a preschool in your community. The teacher asks you to create a new game or activity that the children can play on rainy days. Describe the main features of the game. Is the game appropriate for the cognitive and social abilities of preschool children? Why or why not?

Research

Vivian Gussin Paley's work may be considered participant-observation research because she interacts with the children and observes their behavior. List two advantages and two disadvantages of this approach. Do the advantages outweigh the disadvantages, or vice versa? Why? Briefly describe another approach Paley might use to study the cognitive and social development of preschool children.

FANTASY AND STORYTELLING: CHILDREN AT PLAY

Harry Crews

Developmental Concepts
dramatic play, family and cultural influences

Writer Harry Crews, who grew up in Georgia the son of a poor farmer, remembers playing with children whose parents worked the same land as his father did. Money was scarce. Toys were made out of empty tobacco cans and old Sears catalogs. The catalogs had many uses: they were sometimes a "Wish Book," magical and wondrous, and sometimes a catalyst for telling stories about the models. Their stories show the savvy of these young children as they weave harsh reality into the lives of the two-dimensional figures.

This story opens with Harry Crews remembering when he was five years old and he and his friends Willalee and Lottie Mae used a form of dramatic play to understand the complexities of their families' lives and the hard times in which they lived.

[Auntie Grandma] was full of stories, which, when she had the time—and she usually did—she told to me and Willalee and his little sister, whose name was Lottie Mae. Willalee and my brother and I called her Snottie Mae, but she didn't seem to mind. She came out of the front door when she heard us coming up on the porch and right away wanted to know if she could play in the book with us. She was the same age as I and sometimes we let her play with us, but most of the time we did not. . . .

"Bring us the book," I said.

"I git it for you," she said, "if you give me five of them worms." . . .

She had already seen the two Prince Albert cans full of green worms because Willalee was sitting on the floor now, the lids of the cans open and the worms crawling out. He was lining two of them up for a race from one crack in the floor to the next crack, and he was arranging the rest of the worms in little designs of diamonds and triangles in some game he had not yet discovered the rules for.

"You bring the book," I said, "and you can have two of them worms."

Willalee almost never argued with what I decided to do, up to and including giving away the worms he had spent all morning collecting in the fierce summer heat, which is probably why I liked him so much. Lottie Mae went back into the house and got the Sears, Roebuck catalogue and brought it out onto the porch. He handed her the two worms and told her to go on back in the house, told her it weren't fitting for her to be out here playing with worms while Auntie was back in the kitchen working.

"Ain't nothing left for me to do but put them plates on the table," she said.

"See to them plates then," Willalee said. As young as she was, Lottie Mae had things to do about the place. Whatever she could manage. We all did.

Willalee and I stayed there on the floor with the Sears, Roebuck catalogue and the open Prince Albert cans, out of which deliciously fat worms crawled. Then we opened the catalogue at random as we always did, to see what magic was waiting for us there. . . .

The Sears, Roebuck catalogue was . . . used as a Wish Book, which it was called by the people out in the country, who would never be able to order anything out of it, but could at their leisure spend hours dreaming over.

Willalee Bookatee and I used it for another reason. We made up stories out of it, used it to spin a web of fantasy about us. Without that catalogue our childhood would have been radically different. The federal government ought to strike a medal for the Sears, Roebuck company for sending all those catalogues to farming families, for bringing all that color and all that mystery and all that beauty into the lives of country people.

I first became fascinated with the Sears catalogue because all the people in its pages were perfect. Nearly everybody I knew had something missing, a finger cut off, a toe split, an ear half-chewed away, an eye clouded with blindness from a glancing fence staple. And if they didn't have something missing, they were carry-ing scars from barbed wire, or knives, or fishhooks. But the people in the catalogue had no such hurts. They were not only whole, had all their arms and legs and toes and eyes on their unscarred bodies, but they were also beautiful. Their legs were straight and their heads were never bald and on their faces were looks of happi-ness, even joy, looks that I never saw much of in the faces of the people around me.

Young as I was, though, I had known for a long time that it was all a lie. I knew that under those fancy clothes there had to be scars, there had to be swellings and boils of one kind or another because there was no other way to live in the world. And more than that, at some previous, unremembered moment, I had decided that all the people in the catalogue were related, not necessarily blood kin, but knew one another, and because they knew one another there had to be hard feelings, trouble between them off and on, violence, and hate between them as well as love. And it was out of this knowledge that I first began to make up stories about the peo-ple I found in the book.

Once I began to make up stories about them, Willalee and Lottie Mae began to make up stories, too. The stories they made up were every bit as good as mine. Sometimes better. More than once we had spent whole rainy afternoons when it was too wet to go to the field turning the pages of the catalogue, forcing the beautiful people to give up the secrets of their lives: how they felt about one another, what kind of sicknesses they may have had, what kind of scars they carried in their flesh under all those bright and fancy clothes.

Willalee had his pocketknife out and was about to operate on one of the green cutworms because he liked to pretend he was a doctor. It was I who first put the notion in his head that he might in fact be a doctor, and since we almost never saw a doctor and because they were mysterious and always drove cars or else fine buggies behind high-stepping mares, quickly healing people with their secret medicines, the notion stuck in Willalee's head, and he became very good at taking cutworms and other things apart with his pocketknife.

The Sears catalogue that we had opened at random found a man in his middle years but still strong and healthy with a head full of hair and clear, direct eyes looking out at us, dressed in a red hunting jacket and wading boots, with a rack of shotguns behind him. We used our fingers to mark the spot and turned the Wish Book again, and this time it opened to ladies standing in their underwear, lovely as none we had ever seen, all perfect in their unstained clothes. Every last one of them had the same direct and steady eyes of the man in the red hunting jacket.

I said: "What do you think, Willalee?"

Without hesitation, Willalee said: "This lady here in her step-ins is his chile."

We kept the spot marked with the lady in the step-ins and the man in the hunting jacket and turned the book again, and there was a young man in a suit, the creases sharp enough to shave with, posed with his foot casually propped on a box, every strand of his beautiful hair in place.

"See, what it is," I said. "This boy right here is seeing that girl back there, the one in her step-ins, and she is the youngun of him back there, and them shotguns behind'm belong to him, and he ain't happy."

"Why he ain't happy?"

"Cause this feller standing here in this suit looking so nice, he ain't nice at all. He's mean, but he don't look mean. That gal is the only youngun the feller in the jacket's got, and he loves her cause she is a sweet child. He don't want her fooling with that sorry man in that suit. He's so sorry he done got hisself in trouble with the law. The high sheriff is looking for him right now. Him in the suit will fool around on you."

"How it is he fool around?"

"He'll steal anything he can put his hand to," I said. "He'll steal your hog, or he'll steal your cow out of your field. He's so sorry he'll take that cow if it's the only cow you got. It's just the kind of feller he is."

Willalee said: "Then how come it is she mess around with him?"

"That suit," I said, "done turned that young girl's head. Daddy always says if you give a man a white shirt and a tie and a suit of clothes, you can find out real quick how sorry he is. Daddy says it's the quickest way to find out."

"Do her daddy know she's messing round with him?"

"Shore he knows. A man allus knows what his younggun is doing. Special if she's a girl." I flipped back to the man in the red hunting jacket and the wading boots. "You see them shotguns behind him there on the wall? Them his guns. That second one right there, see that one, the double barrel? That gun is loaded with double-ought buckshot. You know how come it loaded?"

"He gone stop that fooling around," said Willalee.

And so we sat there on the porch with the pots and pans banging back in the house over the iron stove and Lottie Mae there in the door where she had come to stand and listen to us as we talked even though we would not let her help with the story. And before it was over, we had discovered all the connections possible between the girl in the step-ins and the young man in the knife-creased suit and the older man in the red hunting jacket with the shotguns on the wall behind him. And more than that we also discovered that the man's kin people, when they had found out about the trouble he was having with his daughter and the young man, had plans of their own to fix it so the high sheriff wouldn't even have to know about it. They were going to set up and wait on him to take a shoat hog out of another field, and when he did, they'd be waiting with their own guns and knives (which we stumbled upon in another part of the catalogue) and they was gonna throw down on him and see if they couldn't make two pieces out of him instead of one. We had in the story what they thought and what they said and what they felt and why they didn't think that the young man, as good as he looked and as well as he stood in his fancy clothes, would ever straighten out and become the man the daddy wanted for his only daughter.

Before it was over, we even had the girl in the step-ins fixing it so that the boy in the suit could be shot. And by the time my family and Willalee's family came walking down the road from the tobacco field toward the house, the entire Wish Book was filled with feuds of every kind and violence, maimings, and all the other vicious happenings of the world.

Since where we lived and how we lived was almost hermetically sealed from everything and everybody else, fabrication became a way of life. Making up stories, it seems to me now, was not only a way for us to understand the way we lived but also a defense against it. It was no doubt the first step in a life devoted primarily to men and women and children who never lived anywhere but in my imagination. I have found in them infinitely more order and beauty and satisfaction than I ever have in the people who move about me in the real world. And Willalee Bookatee and his family were always there with me in those first tentative steps. God knows what it would have been like if it had not been for Willalee and his people, with whom I spent nearly as much time as I did with my own family. . . .

Response and Analysis

1. Harry Crews describes the imaginative play in which he and his friends engage. What purposes or functions does their playing serve? What does he mean when he says that "making up stories . . . was not only a way for us to understand the way we lived but also a defense against it"? What themes about adult relationships emerge in the children's stories?

2. Briefly describe some of the make-believe games that you played as a child. Did you play them alone or with others? What made the games interesting and fun for you? What might you have learned or mastered in such play?

3. Television was not available to Crews as a child, but it is a major source of information about adult behavior for children today. Do you think that children who watch a lot of television have different conceptions about adult relationships than those who only watch a little television? Why or why not? What types of conceptions might each group have? What information about adult relationships did you learn from watching television?

Research

Crews's article raises important questions about the influence of various media (from catalogs to television, for example) on development. Suppose you are interested in the effects of television violence on children. You decide to conduct a study to examine the amount of violence in children's television programming. You will watch a sample of television shows and record the amount of violence in each show. Before conducting the study, however, you must resolve several key issues: How will you select the programs to watch? Will you watch more than one episode of each program? What criteria will you use to determine whether a character acted in a violent way? How can you be sure that your expectations of violence do not bias your (a) decision about how to conduct the study, (b) observations during the study, or (c) conclusions?

ANGELA'S ASHES: MEMOIR OF A CHILDHOOD

Frank McCourt

Developmental Concepts
poverty; family, community, and cultural factors
influencing development

In his memoir about growing up in America and Ireland, Pulitzer Prize–winning author Frank McCourt wonders how he survived. Here, McCourt describes the devastating impact that extreme poverty had on him and his family. Because his father was often out of work or sometimes drank away the money he did manage to earn, there was little food or medicine for the children. Often the family lived on public assistance and had to accept the help of neighbors and relatives; on occasion, young Frank stole food. Observe how McCourt, the oldest child at age four, was treated and expected to behave when his father didn't come home because of drinking bouts. Note, too, his reactions to his father whom he sees as being three different people: the one in the morning who read to him, the one at night who told stories and said prayers, and the one who did "the bad thing." His "real father," McCourt writes, was the one who lit the fire, made tea, sang, and read quietly to his son so as not to wake the others.

I'm in the playground with Malachy. I'm four, he's three. He lets me push him on the swing because he's no good at swinging himself and Freddie Leibowitz is in school. We have to stay in the playground because the twins are sleeping and my mother says she's worn out. Go out and play, she says, and give me some rest. Dad is out looking for a job again and sometimes he comes home with the smell of whiskey, singing all the songs about suffering Ireland. Mam gets angry and says Ireland can kiss her arse. He says that's nice language to be using in front of the children and she says never mind the language, food on the table is what she wants, not suffering Ireland. . . .

When Dad brings home the first week's wages Mam is delighted she can pay the lovely Italian man in the grocery shop and she can hold her head up again because there's nothing worse in the world than to owe and be beholden to anyone. She cleans the kitchen, washes the mugs and plates, brushes crumbs and bits of food from the table, cleans out the icebox and orders a fresh block of ice from another Italian. She buys toilet paper that we can take down the hall to the lavatory and that, she says, is better than having the headlines from the *Daily News* blackening your arse. She boils water on the stove and spends a day at a great tin tub washing our shirts and socks, diapers for the twins, our two sheets, our three towels. She hangs everything out on the clotheslines behind the apartment house and we can watch the clothes dance in wind and sun. She says you wouldn't want the neighbors to know what you have in the way of a wash but there's nothing like the sweetness of clothes dried by the sun.

When Dad brings home the first week's wages on a Friday night we know the weekend will be wonderful. On Saturday night Mam will boil water on the stove and wash us in the great tin tub and Dad will dry us. Malachy will turn around and show his behind. Dad will pretend to be shocked and we'll all laugh. Mam will make hot cocoa and we'll be able to stay up while Dad tells us a story out of his head. All we have to do is say a name, Mr. MacAdorey or Mr. Leibowitz down the hall, and Dad will have the two of them rowing up a river in Brazil chased by Indians with green noses and puce shoulders. On nights like that we can drift off to sleep knowing there will be a breakfast of eggs, fried tomatoes and fried bread, tea with lashings of sugar and milk and, later in the day, a big dinner of mashed potatoes, peas and ham, and a trifle Mam makes, layers of fruit and warm delicious custard on a cake soaked in sherry. . . .

When Dad's job goes into the third week he does not bring home the wages. On Friday night we wait for him and Mam gives us bread and tea. The darkness comes down and the lights come on along Classon Avenue. Other men with jobs are home already and having eggs for dinner because you can't have meat on a Friday. You can hear the families talking upstairs and downstairs and down the hall and Bing Crosby is singing on the radio, Brother, can you spare a dime? . . .

On the morning of the fourth Friday of Dad's job Mam asks him if he'll be home tonight with his wages or will he drink everything again? He looks at us and shakes his head at Mam as if to say, Och, you shouldn't talk like that in front of the children.

Mam keeps at him. I'm asking you, Are you coming home so that we can have a bit of supper or will it be midnight with no money in your pocket and you singing Kevin Barry and the rest of the sad songs?

He puts on his cap, shoves his hands into his trouser pockets, sighs and looks up at the ceiling. I told you before I'll be home, he says.

Later in the day Mam dresses us. She puts the twins into the pram[1] and off we go through the long streets of Brooklyn. Sometimes she lets Malachy sit in the pram when he's tired of trotting along beside her. She tells me I'm too big for the pram. I could tell her I have pains in my legs from trying to keep up with her but she's not singing and I know this is not the day to be talking about my pains.

---

[1]pram: baby carriage.

We come to a big gate where there's a man standing in a box with windows all around. Mam talks to the man. She wants to know if she can go inside to where the men are paid and maybe they'd give her some of Dad's wages so he wouldn't spend it in the bars. The man shakes his head. I'm sorry, lady, but if we did that we'd have half the wives in Brooklyn storming the place. Lotta men have the drinking problem but there's nothing we can do long as they show up sober and do their work.

We wait across the street. Mam lets me sit on the sidewalk with my back against the wall. She gives the twins their bottles of water and sugar but Malachy and I have to wait till she gets money from Dad and we can go to the Italian for tea and bread and eggs.

When the whistle blows . . . men in caps and overalls swarm through the gate, their faces and hands black from the work. Mam tells us watch carefully for Dad because she can hardly see across the street herself, her eyes are that bad. There are dozens of men, then a few, then none. Mam is crying, Why couldn't ye see him? Are ye blind or what?

She goes back to the man in the box. Are you sure there wouldn't be one man left inside?

No, lady, he says. They're out. I don't know how he got past you.

We go back through the long streets of Brooklyn. The twins hold up their bottles and cry for more water and sugar. Malachy says he's hungry and Mam tells him wait a little, we'll get money from Dad and we'll all have a nice supper. We'll go to the Italian and get eggs and make toast with the flames on the stove and we'll have jam on it. Oh, we will, and we'll all be nice and warm.

It's dark on Atlantic Avenue and all the bars around the Long Island Railroad Station are bright and noisy. We go from bar to bar looking for Dad. Mam leaves us outside with the pram while she goes in or she sends me. There are crowds of noisy men and stale smells that remind me of Dad when he comes home with the smell of the whiskey on him.

The man behind the bar says, Yeah, sonny, whaddya want? You're not supposeta be in here, y'know.

I'm looking for my father. Is my father here?

Naw, sonny, how'd I know dat? Who's your fawdah?

His name is Malachy and he sings Kevin Barry.

Malarkey?

No, Malachy.

Malachy? And he sings Kevin Barry?

He calls out to the men in the bar, Youse guys, youse know guy Malachy what sings Kevin Barry?

Men shake their heads. One says he knew a guy Michael sang Kevin Barry but he died of the drink which he had because of his war wounds. . . .

Mam tries all the bars around the station before she gives up. She leans against a wall and cries. Jesus, we still have to walk all the way to Classon Avenue and I have four starving children. She sends me back into the bar . . . to see if the barman would fill the twins' bottles with water and maybe a little sugar in each. The men in the bar think it's very funny that the barman should be filling baby bottles but he's big and he tells them shut their lip. He tells me babies should be drinking milk not water and when I tell him Mam doesn't have the money he empties the baby bottles and fills them with milk. He says, Tell ya mom they need that for the teeth an' bones. Ya drink water an' sugar an' all ya get is rickets. Tell ya Mom.

Mam is happy with the milk. She says she knows all about teeth and bones and rickets but beggars can't be choosers.

When we reach Classon Avenue she goes straight to the Italian grocery shop. She tells the man her husband is late tonight, that he's probably working overtime, and would it be at all possible to get a few things and she'll be sure to see him tomorrow?

The Italian says, Missus, you always pay your bill sooner or later and you can have anything you like in this store.

Oh, she says, I don't want much.

Anything you like, missus, because I know you're an honest woman and you got a bunch o' nice kids there.

We have eggs and toast and jam though we're so weary walking the long streets of Brooklyn we can barely move our jaws to chew. The twins fall asleep after eating and Mam lays them on the bed to change their diapers. She sends me down the hall to rinse the dirty diapers in the lavatory so that they can be hung up to dry and used the next day. Malachy helps her wash the twins' bottoms though he's ready to fall asleep himself.

I crawl into bed with Malachy and the twins. I look out at Mam at the kitchen table, smoking a cigarette, drinking tea, and crying. I want to get up and tell her I'll be a man soon and I'll get a job in the place with the big gate and I'll come home every Friday night with money for eggs and toast and jam and she can sing again Anyone can see why I wanted your kiss.

The next week Dad loses the job. He comes home that Friday night, throws his wages on the table and says to Mam, Are you happy now? You hang around the gate complaining and accusing and they sack me. They were looking for an excuse and you gave it to them.

He takes a few dollars from his wages and goes out. He comes home late roaring and singing. The twins cry and Mam shushes them and cries a long time herself.

When Frank McCourt was four years old, his family moved from the United States to Ireland. His father struggled to find and hold a job, and he continued to drink. The McCourts had lost three children under five years of age: Margaret in America and the twins in Ireland. In the next segment, McCourt tells about his relationship with his father and his feelings about his father's drinking.

I know when Dad does the bad thing. I know when he drinks the dole money and Mam is desperate and has to beg at the St. Vincent de Paul Society and ask for credit at Kathleen O'Connell's shop but I don't want to back away from him and run to Mam. How can I do that when I'm up with him early every morning with the whole world asleep? He lights the fire and makes the tea and sings to himself or reads the paper to me in a whisper that won't wake up the rest of the family. . . .

He gets the *Irish Press* early and tells me about the world, Hitler, Mussolini, Franco. He says, this war is none of our business because the English are up to their tricks again. He tells me about the great Roosevelt in Washington and the great de Valera in Dublin. In the morning we have the world to ourselves and he never tells me I should die for Ireland. . . .

Before bed we sit around the fire and if we say, Dad, tell us a story, he makes up one about someone in the lane and the story will take us all over the world, up in the air, under the sea and back to the lane. Everyone in the story is a different color and everything is upside down and backward. Motor cars and planes go under water and submarines fly through the air. Sharks sit in trees and giant salmon sport with kangaroos on the moon. Polar bears wrestle with elephants in Australia and penguins teach Zulus how to play bagpipes. After the story he takes us upstairs and kneels with us while we say our prayers. We say the Our Father, three Hail Marys, God bless the Pope. God bless Mam, God bless our dead sister and brothers, God bless Ireland, God bless de Valera, and God bless anyone who gives Dad a job. He says, Go to sleep, boys, because holy God is watching you and He always knows if you're not good.

I think my father is like the Holy Trinity with three people in him, the one in the morning with the paper, the one at night with the stories and the prayers, and then the one who does the bad thing and comes home with the smell of whiskey and wants us to die for Ireland.

I feel sad over the bad thing but I can't back away from him because the one in the morning is my real father and if I were in America I could say, I love you, Dad, the way they do in the films, but you can't say that in Limerick for fear you might be laughed at. You're allowed to say you love God and babies and horses that win but anything else is a softness in the head.

Response and Analysis

1. What parental functions does Frank McCourt's father relinquish? Which does his mother relinquish? When does she do so? What parental functions does young Frank McCourt undertake? How might taking on such responsibilities affect a four-year-old child? Describe the adult-like thinking that young McCourt engages in?

2. As a boy, McCourt was able to hold contradictory images of his father in his mind. How does his ability to see his father as some- times good and sometimes bad help him cope with the family dysfunction? Suppose McCourt had seen his father as all bad. How might that view have affected the boy's psychological development? His relationship with his father?

3. McCourt (who lived in Ireland from about age four to age nineteen) believes that American families (which he knew in his youth mostly from the movies) freely say "I love you" and show affection more often than Irish families. Why is it important for

family members to tell one another of their love?

Research

Suppose that you are interested in examining why some children who grow up in dysfunctional environments become alcoholics, criminals, or develop psychological disorders, whereas others excel in school and become successful high-functioning adults. You decide to conduct a fifteen-year longitudinal study on this question. The sample includes one hundred families who have at least one child under the age of eight. You interview each family member every six months for the next fifteen years. Unfortunately, during the study 60 percent of the participants move out of the area and discontinue their participation. How might the loss of these participants affect your conclusions?

NIGHT VISITORS: IMAGINATION OR REALITY?

Annie Dillard

Developmental Concepts
imagination, reality testing, problem solving

When Annie Dillard was a child, almost everything she saw was full of mystery to be explored and solved. Here she recalls an incident that has stayed with her since she was five years old. As she lay in bed surrounded by darkness, she would wait for sleep to come. What came, on many nights, however, were mysterious figures streaking across the walls—"night visitors"—whose presence she could not account for. Would they cause harm, she wondered? How did they get into her room? What took place in the world outside that seemed to encroach into her home? Preschoolers begin to develop basic problem-solving skills, and young Annie eventually solves the puzzle.

When I was five, growing up in Pittsburgh . . . I would not go to bed willingly because something came into my room. This was a private matter between me and it. If I spoke of it, it would kill me.

Who could breathe as this thing searched for me over the very corners of the room? Who could ever breathe freely again? I lay in the dark.

My sister Amy, two years old, was asleep in the other bed. What did she know? She was innocent of evil. Even at two she composed herself attractively for sleep. She folded the top sheet tidily under her prettily outstretched arm; she laid her perfect head lightly on an unwrinkled pillow, where her thick curls spread evenly in rays like petals. All night long she slept smoothly in a series of pleasant and serene, if artificial-looking, positions, a faint smile on her closed lips, as if she were posing for an ad for sheets. There was no messiness in her, no roughness for things to cling to, only a charming and charmed innocence that seemed then to protect her, an innocence I needed but couldn't muster. Since Amy was asleep, furthermore, and since when I needed someone most I was afraid to stir enough to wake her, she was useless.

I lay alone and was almost asleep when the damned thing entered the room by flattening itself against the open door and sliding in. It was a transparent, luminous oblong. I could see the door whiten at its touch; I could see the blue wall turn pale where it raced over it, and see the maple headboard of Amy's bed glow. It was a swift spirit; it was an awareness. It made noise. It had two joined parts, a head and a tail, like a Chinese dragon. It found the door, wall, and headboard; and it swiped them, charging them with its luminous glance. After its fleet, searching passage, things looked the same, but weren't.

I dared not blink or breathe; I tried to hush my whooping blood. If it found another awareness, it would destroy it.

Every night before it got to me it gave up. It hit my wall's corner and couldn't get past. It shrank completely into itself and vanished like a cobra down a hole. I heard the rising roar it made when it died or left. I still couldn't breathe. I knew—it was the worst fact I knew, a very hard fact—that it could return again alive that same night.

Sometimes it came back, sometimes it didn't. Most often, restless, it came back. The light stripe slipped in the door, ran searching over Amy's wall, stopped, stretched lunatic at the first corner, raced wailing toward my wall, and vanished into the second corner with a cry. So I wouldn't go to bed.

It was a passing car whose windshield reflected the corner streetlight outside. I figured it out one night.

Figuring it out was as memorable as the oblong itself. Figuring it out was a long and forced ascent to the very rim of being, to the membrane of skin that both separates and connects the inner life and the outer world. I climbed deliberately from the depths like a diver who releases the monster in his arms and hauls himself hand over hand up an anchor chain till he meets the ocean's sparkling membrane and bursts through it; he sights the sunlit, becalmed hull of his boat, which had bulked so ominously from below.

I recognized the noise it made when it left. That is, the noise it made called to mind, at last, my daytime sensations when a car passed—the sight and noise together. A car came roaring down hushed Edgerton Avenue in front of our house, stopped at the corner stop sign, and passed on shrieking as its engine shifted up the gears. What, precisely, came into the bedroom? A reflection from the car's oblong windshield. Why did it travel in two parts? The window sash split the light and cast a shadow.

Night after night I labored up the same long chain of reasoning, as night after night the thing burst into the room where I lay awake and Amy slept prettily and my loud heart thrashed and I froze.

There was a world outside my window and contiguous to it. If I was so all-fired bright, as my parents, who had patently no basis for comparison, seemed to think, why did I have to keep learning this same thing over and over? For I had learned it a summer ago, when men with jackhammers broke up Edgerton Avenue. I had watched them from the yard; the street came up in jagged slabs like floes. When I lay to nap, I listened. One restless afternoon I connected the new noise in my bedroom with the jackhammer men I had been seeing outside. I understood abruptly that these worlds met, the outside and the inside. I traveled the route in my mind: You walked downstairs from here, and outside from downstairs. "Outside," then, was conceivably just beyond my windows. It was the same world I reached by going out the front or the back door. I forced my imagination yet again over this route.

The world did not have me in mind; it had no mind. It was a coincidental collection of things and people, of items, and I myself was one such item—a child walking up the sidewalk, whom anyone could see or ignore. The things in the world did not necessarily cause my overwhelming feelings; the feelings were inside me, beneath my skin, behind my ribs, within my skull. They were even, to some extent, under my control.

I could be connected to the outer world by reason, if I chose, or I could yield to what amounted to a narrative fiction, to a tale of terror whispered to me by the blood in my ears, a show in light projected on the room's blue walls. As time passed, I learned to amuse myself in bed in the darkened room by entering the fiction deliberately and replacing it by reason deliberately.

When the low roar drew nigh and the oblong slid in the door, I threw my own switches for pleasure. It's coming after me; it's a car outside. It's after me. It's a car. It raced over the wall, lighting it blue wherever it ran; it bumped over Amy's maple headboard in a rush, paused, slithered elongate over the corner, shrank, flew my way, and vanished into itself with a wail. It was a car.

Response and Analysis

1. Annie Dillard contrasts the peaceful sleep of her younger, two-year-old sister with her own more troubled sleep. What differences in cognitive development might account for the ease with which Dillard's sister falls asleep and for her sister's lack of appreciation for Dillard's nighttime fears?

2. Give an example of egocentrism from Dillard's story. How does egocentrism correspond to Piaget's ideas about cognitive development at the preoperational stage?

3. How does Dillard discover the cause of the "transparent, luminous oblong" she fears? How does she associate the mysterious figure on the wall with the outside world? Why is the discovery meaningful for Dillard?

4. Recall a childhood fear that you (or someone you know) once had. In what ways might the fear have reflected childhood egocentrism? What events or objects might have started the fear? How might an adult have helped you (or the other person) cope with the fear?

Research

Changes in one area of development (for example, cognitive) often affect other areas (for example, psychosocial). How might changes in egocentrism (in the cognitive domain) affect psychosocial development? For example, how might becoming less egocentric affect a child's peer relationships or a child's ability to empathize and manage interpersonal conflict? State your answer to this question in the form of a hypothesis.

COPING WITH ATTENTION-DEFICIT/ HYPERACTIVITY DISORDER

Ann Colin

Developmental Concepts
attention-deficit/hyperactivity disorder (formerly called attention-deficit disorder), behavior problems, parenting skills

Children who suffer from attention-deficit/hyperactivity disorder (ADHD) are often easily distracted, have difficulty concentrating for a period of time, are often disorganized, and frequently react impulsively. Ann Colin experienced frustration with her four-year-old son, Willie, who suffers from this disorder. When prescription drugs did not help, Colin found a cognitive therapist who was willing to work with her son to help him reduce his level of frustration. Colin describes Willie's behavior before and after treatment, and she is now hopeful that the family will be better able to handle difficulties that her son may have in the future.

January 30, 1994

It's another blustery Saturday, and Willie, our towheaded four-year-old, is raging as if the winter storm outside has moved into his body. Unlike most children with attention-deficit disorder (ADD), Willie has not been helped by Ritalin, the medication commonly prescribed—perhaps because he's too young. For the past week he's been trying Dexedrine, a pharmaceutical cousin of Ritalin. Although the pills are supposed to help Willie feel less impulsive and emotional, as we're eating, he suddenly becomes furious.

"I wanted Aladdin, not Jasmine," he explodes, holding up the plastic princess that came from McDonald's.

"I'm sorry, sweetheart, they're not giving out Aladdin this week. Should we put it on the list?"

To help avoid temper tantrums when Willie wants something that we can't give him, Dr. Andersov, the psychologist we've been consulting, has suggested keeping a list of desired items he can earn with good behavior. If he still gets angry, she's told us that we should give him some time to cool down on his own.

"Come on, Willie," I say. "Let's cool down."

"No!" he shrieks. "I want Aladdin!" Willie howls, his face turning red. This is well beyond the scope of a typical preschooler's outbursts. My son's hands are balled into tight little fists. His back is rigid, a braid of anger and adrenaline.

When I try to stroke his hand, he swings around and scratches me. Two red marks well up on my wrist. I'm so astonished, all I can do is grab him and pull him into his room. So much for our cooldown. I'm white-hot and Willie is howling.

"No, no! I don't want to go," he's shouting.

"You scratched me," I say. "That's not okay."

I put him in his room, slamming the door behind me. "You can come out when you're ready to follow the rules of the house," I hear myself saying firmly. I'm mad—furious, really—but I don't want to raise the stakes by getting into a screaming match.

"I won't stay here," Willie shouts from inside his room. "I'm going to escape. I'm going to get a match and set the house on fire. . . ."

He pulls at the door, which I'm holding closed as hard as I can. We don't have an outside latch on this door—we had never thought we'd need one. After all these doctors and medicines and specialists, I feel like we're worse off than we were a year ago, when Willie first got the tentative ADD diagnosis at age three. While some experts believe ADD can't be diagnosed until a child is age five or six, Dr. Andersov felt Willie's symptoms showed all the markings of classic ADD . . . I can't believe how awful the scene is: Willie butting against the door like a caged bull, me the grimacing monster making him a prisoner.

Willie continues to hurl his body against the door. What's going to happen when he gets too big for me to handle? Already it's hard for me to carry him up the stairs.

The movement stops on his side of the door, and I pray that he has just worn himself out. I'm about to let go of the handle when I hear the huge crash of something against the door. Something solid and large—a chair, maybe.

"Willie!" I scream. "That is enough!"

"I'll teach you," Willie howls. "I'm going to kill myself. I'm going to run away and never come back, and then you'll be sad forever!"

I make a mental inventory of what's in his room, if there's anything sharp he could hurt himself with. I can't believe this is my own sweet child in there. I wish I could wake up and find this has all been a bad dream.

Clutching the door handle as if it were a safety raft, I'm in a panic. *Don't engage him; don't enrage him.* Dr. Andersov's words ring in my ears like a mantra. My own breathing sounds deafening to me, huge waves of oxygen that seem to bring no air.

A few minutes pass and I hear nothing from inside. After a few more, I release the doorknob. Willie seems to have calmed down, though I'm a nervous wreck.

I walk downstairs and am grateful to see my husband, Peter, who has just come home. "What are we going to do?" I ask him. "This medicine isn't working either."

Suddenly we hear the skittering of little feet on the stairs—Willie making his escape. "Mom," he says softly, "can I come out now?"

"Are you ready to follow the rules of the house?"

"Yes, Mommy. I'm sorry I scratched you." He hugs me and I pull him close.

I don't know if I can take any more scenes like this. What if Willie impulsively hurts himself or somebody else? Peter and I stare at each other helplessly. We know we've got to do something.

February 6, 1994

Since the drugs haven't helped and Willie's behavior has been so alarming, Dr. Andersov agrees that he's ready for cognitive therapy; we had held off on it until now because we were told he was too young. Willie will start seeing Dr. Andersov once a week, and I'll act as what she calls a "cotherapist." We'll mostly play with toys in her office in order to re-create some of the difficult situations he encounters at school.

It's a huge time commitment and means more hours for Jolie, our baby-sitter, who'll have to take care of our two-year-old son, Nicholas, while Willie and I are at Dr. Andersov's. It's also expensive, given that my career as a freelance writer doesn't produce regular paychecks and our family's health insurance pays only half the cost of each office visit. What choice do we have, though? This is our only hope.

March 9, 1994

The director of Willie's nursery school is calling frequently, concerned about Willie's behavior. Peter and I spend as much time in the classroom as we can, trying to help Willie negotiate better with the other kids, but he is still easily frustrated and aggressive. In the block corner, for example, Willie might knock down another child's building or hit his classmates to get what he wants. He also can't stand to be teased, not even the mild, joking kind that's typical of the way many preschoolers communicate with each other. I keep reminding myself that this is a boy who thanks us repeatedly for giving him a bubble bath. Why can't his endearing side come out in school?

The director says she's hopeful that Willie can stay in the class, but he needs to have an extra adult with him each morning during free play, circle time, and gym—his hardest activities. She's recommending we hire a graduate student to be what she calls a "shadow," as it's not really practical or desirable for Peter and me to fill that role.

I suppose I should be grateful they're not kicking him out, but I'm worried about the expense of a shadow because it's not covered by our insurance. There are extra "floater" teachers on call, but the director says she needs to keep them free for emergencies. (If this isn't an emergency, I wonder, what is?)

April 11, 1994

The goal of our therapy is to stretch Willie's tolerance of frustration, so he'll be better able to play games according to other kids' rules. Dr. Andersov also wants to help him understand the difference between "mean" and simply silly teasing. If he can handle a little at a time with us in her office, he should be able to deal with more on his own at school.

Today he dumps about two dozen green plastic soldiers out of a plastic bag onto the sand table and starts lining them up, making two armies in a face-off. Willie usually insists that I be on his, the "good-guy," team.

"But I want to be on the bad-guy team," I say, arching my eyebrows like a cartoon villain. I make a face as if I've just smelled something awful. "Yuck," I say. "I'm stinky, like a dirty diaper."

Willie's eyes are wide with delight and shock. He seems to see that if I can tease myself, it must not be so bad to occasionally get called a name, especially if it's such a funny one.

"Now, it doesn't hurt your mom to be called a dirty diaper—right, Willie?" Dr. Andersov says.

"No. . . ." he acknowledges, cautiously. "It's just funny teasing."

"I'm so stinky," I say, pretending to sniff myself. "You better not be on my team."

"Okay," he says, gamely. "I'm on the other team and you're with the stinky, dirty diapers."

"Ughhh," Willie says, knocking over one of his men dramatically. "You killed me with your stinky smell." Score one for the dirty-diaper team. I guess.

August 24, 1994

We're on vacation in Massachusetts, and the boys are having a ball, catching frogs all day and eating ice-cream sandwiches on the porch after dinner. Willie begs me to take him swimming at a nearby lake.

Only a few kids are left on the beach when we arrive, digging long canals in the sand. Willie crouches down, watching them, trying to figure out their game and how he can be a part of it. The fact that Willie understands he needs to negotiate an invitation is a big step for him, the kind of specific skill building we had been working on all spring at Dr. Andersov's.

"Excuse me," Willie says to the oldest child. "Your game looks cool. Can I play with ya'?"

The boy turns and shrugs as if it's the most natural thing in the world that Willie would join them.

"Okay, get water," he says.

Willie grabs his bucket and is about to run to the lake when he wheels around and beams at me, giving me a giant thumbs-up.

September 13, 1994

Today is Willie's first day at his new school, and we're all so excited that we're ten minutes early for the bus. Though his preschool never formally asked him to leave, it was clear that they were unwilling to have him continue on to kindergarten without a shadow, and we wanted him to be in a class where he could manage on his own.

Picking a place for him was a real challenge. Peter and I looked at regular schools, but realized we needed to investigate programs designed for kids with learning or behavioral differences. The special-ed program in our local public school was overenrolled, so we chose a private school. The tuition is steep, but we'll be able to deduct it as a medical expense on our taxes.

The classes are small: eight students with two teachers. Behavior and reading specialists are also on staff. I have a good feeling about this. I think we're finally with a place that will appreciate Willie for who he is.

December 20, 1994

Remarkably, Willie's teacher, Mrs. Rose, has told us that he's a pleasure to have in class. There have been no tantrums or shouting, and we know from his busy calendar of playdates and birthday parties that he's made lots of friends. Yet I was still astonished when Dr. Andersov told us last month that we could start winding down Willie's therapy.

Today is his "graduation" day. Dr. Andersov looks almost as proud as I feel. I look at the sand table and soft maroon carpet where I've spent ten months of weekly visits with Willie. He's grinning from ear to ear at his going-away celebration. Dr. Andersov has brought cookies, and he munches away happily as he draws with his markers.

Although she's told me that her door is always open to us, it's almost unimaginable to me that we're not going to be spending this intense, revelatory time together every week. It's been such a privilege to see Willie through all the setbacks and breakthroughs. I've learned so much about the way he thinks.

I pick up one of the markers. "I love you," I write to Willie.

Dr. Andersov writes, "I'll miss you."

Willie reads her note out loud. I don't know what we would have done without her this year. I feel like she's saved Willie's life.

The doorbell rings outside, and Jolie and Nicky, who have come to meet us, enter the waiting room.

"Would you like your brother and baby-sitter to join your graduation party?" Dr. Andersov asks.

"Okay," Willie agrees.

We open the door, and suddenly it seems very crowded inside with Nicky dashing back and forth. "Don't run, Nicky," says Willie, the voice of authority. "I'll help you get the toys."

I glance at my watch, realizing it's almost time to go. Willie hugs Dr. Andersov at the door, and I do too. There's the smell of snow in the air, and the sky is a deep blue-purple. In less than two weeks, it will be a new year.

Willie wants to run ahead and promises me that he'll stop at the corner. I close my eyes and can picture his strong legs moving, a determined look on his face to go faster. Though I know we'll still have issues to deal with as he gets older, I feel confident now that we can work with Willie to handle any challenge. When I open my eyes, there he is, exactly where he promised—panting, exhilarated, waiting for the rest of us.

Response and Analysis

1. What behaviors does Willie exhibit that reflect problems with attention? Hyperactivity? Why might it be important for parents or others to determine whether behavior problems occur in more than one setting? Are Willie's behavior problems present in two or more settings?

2. Many children in middle childhood, especially boys, show signs of limited attention, high activity, and occasional aggressiveness. What criteria would be needed to determine whether a child should be considered as having ADHD as opposed to being highly active or having some other behavior problem? What are the advantages and disadvantages of diagnosing a child as having ADHD?

3. What treatments and therapy techniques did Willie's therapist implement? Why were they effective? Based on your reading of Wil-

lie's experiences, what do you think schools should do to accommodate children with ADHD?

Research

Suppose you are interested in designing a study to examine whether food additives can cause ADHD. In thinking about the study, you realize that you will have to rely on parents' reports to assess children's behavior. You are concerned that the parents may have expectations about the effects of food additives and that these expectations may influence how the parents interpret their child's behavior. For example, parents may "see" more hyperactive behaviors in their child if they believe he or she has just eaten a food containing certain additives. Similarly, parents may report fewer hyperactive behaviors in their child if they believe he or she has just eaten foods that do not contain additives. How might you design the study to avoid these expectations and biases?

section 3

MIDDLE CHILDHOOD

*"What did you find today?" my
grandmother . . . would ask, as she sat
picking at a crust of cockleburrs in one of
my socks. I would run to my mud-stiffened
pants to dig through the pockets for a rock
an Indian might have used, or a leaf I
liked, crumpled and fragrant, or a
waterlogged stick turning into a fossil, a
furry length of twine I had braided from
cedar bark: "I could use this to snare a
rabbit if I had to."*

KIM STAFFORD, *Having Everything Right*

Compared to the rapid development of early childhood and the erratic changes
that come with adolescence, development in middle childhood is relatively smooth
and steady. Play becomes more skill-based as increases in strength and coordination
permit children to enjoy activities that were formerly beyond their abilities, such as
catching a ball, climbing a tree, riding a bike, or practicing in-line skating.
Cognitively, children develop an ability to look at problems from more than one
perspective, so thinking becomes more systematic. Social relations become more
complex, and friendships depend increasingly on expectations of self-disclosure and
mutual support. During the first half of middle childhood (ages six, seven, and eight),
children often show high self-confidence, but some lose a degree of this confidence
as they approach adolescence and become more introspective.

Young Russell Baker is asked to assume adult skills, to become industrious and
productive, before he feels ready to do so. After his father dies, Russell's mother
wants him to become the man of the house. Determined that he should make
something of himself, his mother helps him get a paper route, and then she makes
sure that he follows through. In the course of these lessons, Baker's mother uses

one of the oldest persuasion techniques: spanking. This selection shows some of the pressures on boys to learn gender roles and become men as well as some of the struggles of single mothers trying to raise children.

Nancy Samalin describes some of the complexities of sibling relationships. She notes that petty bickering among siblings often baffles parents, but she reminds us that such bickering is normal and to be expected. Fights over who gets to turn off the television or who has rights to sit in which chair are not precursors to "a lifetime of hatred." Children can move easily between conflict and deep appreciation for their siblings, as their own comments show. Strong loyalties usually develop, and sibling relationships are often among the most resilient in a person's life.

According to projections, the population of the United States will continue to become more culturally diverse in the twenty-first century. English is not the native language for many immigrants, so families, schools, and communities face the challenge of helping children from different backgrounds succeed. Growing up in Sacramento, California, Richard Rodriguez had a bilingual childhood. Once he became proficient in English, Rodriguez found that his relationships with his family and neighborhood changed. He had become an inhabitant of two cultures, but he had difficulty feeling entirely at home in either. Here, Rodriguez explores the subtleties of language and his struggle to develop a more comfortable public identity while still cherishing the intimacy of his home where Spanish was spoken. His ability to recognize and reflect on his thoughts and experiences with language—a process called *metacognition*—greatly aids his coping.

John Philo Dixon recalls how experiences in school affected his life. Dixon had difficulty learning to read, and his inability to keep up with the rest of the class on reading assignments left him feeling inadequate. Many theorists have characterized middle childhood as a stage in which children strive to develop competencies that they will need as adults. Erik Erikson, for example, refers to this period as a crisis of industry versus inferiority—children must learn to do what is important and necessary or face persistent feelings of inadequacy. School is a child's primary arena for developing and demonstrating competence, so Dixon was at risk for problems. Fortunately, he discovered his strength with algebra and later with physics, but it was not until he was in ninth grade that "the long depression of elementary school ended." Dixon's story also raises interesting questions about how schools can facilitate the development of children with special needs.

Annie Dillard, a naturalist with a talent for describing both the inner and outer worlds, recounts an important incident from her middle childhood years. In Section 2, we saw Dillard as a five-year-old coping with imaginary fears, and now we see her in middle childhood applying more developed cognitive skills. She is fascinated by her discovery of an amoeba under a microscope and she wants her parents to share in her excitement. However, they have other interests at the time, and their reaction causes Dillard to realize that "my days and nights were my own to plan and fill." Her description of the incident illustrates how a child's readiness and parents' reactions can combine to begin the transition from the concerns of middle childhood (for example, industriousness) to the concerns of adolescence (for example, identity).

Researcher Martin E. P. Seligman and his colleagues are interested in developing cognitive coping skills and optimism in children. They describe a research project involving fifth- and sixth-graders who were at risk for depression. In addition to illustrating how coping skills can be taught and can help children avoid depression, this selection shows the challenges of conducting research and how research is critical to our understanding of child development.

A YOUNG BOY BECOMES MAN
OF THE HOUSE

Russell Baker

Developmental Concepts
achievement motivation, influence of mother and
single-parent home, discipline styles

When Russell Baker was five years old, his father died unexpectedly at the age of
thirty-three from an acute diabetic coma. Baker's mother was left with three small
children to care for, one of whom she eventually sent to live with a relative. As the
years wore on and his mother's friendship with Oluf, a suitor, failed to turn into a
permanent relationship, young Russell found himself increasingly the focus of her
attention. Baker writes of the determination and force his mother wielded to make
sure that he would "make something of himself." Here he describes the trials he
underwent as an eight-year-old, the punishments he suffered, and the burdens he
carried. Yet Baker's tone is one of resigned understanding, and he did, in fact, fulfill
and no doubt exceed his mother's ambitions for him. For many years, Baker was
a highly respected journalist for the *New York Times* and currently is host of
Masterpiece Theater.

If anyone had told me we were poor, I would have been astounded. We ate well
enough. There was always a bowl of oatmeal at breakfast, a bologna sandwich for
lunch, and a cup of coffee to wash it down. . . .

With so many idle hours at her disposal my mother was focusing all her school-
teacher's energies on perfecting the education I would need to make something of
myself. As a result I was always well ahead of most of the class at school and basked
in a steady flow of A's and gold stars. I think she was already preparing me for the
day when Oluf would secure our future and I would be sent off to college.

When this hope came crashing down that summer, I was totally unaware that
anything terrible had happened to her. It had been a year or more since I had last
seen Oluf. I knew nothing of what had been growing between them in the mails. I
had forgotten Oluf existed, and when he ceased to exist for my mother, too, she
gave me no outward sign that her life had come to another turning point.

At this moment, in her defeat, however, she was already laying plans for another campaign, a longer, harder struggle to come up from the bottom without

help from the sort of Providence Oluf had represented. In this long, hard pull, I was now cast as the central figure. She would spend her middle years turning me into the man who would redeem her failed youth. I would make something of myself, and if *I* lacked the grit to do it, well then *she* would make me make something of myself. I would become the living proof of the strength of her womanhood. From now on she would live for me, and, in turn, I would become her future.

The results of this decision began to appear immediately, though I was only vaguely sensitive to them. Since coming to New Jersey she and Doris[1] and I had slept together, all of us in my father's bed which she had brought from Morrisonville. That summer she put me out of her bed. "It's time you started sleeping by yourself," she said. After that I slept on a couch in the parlor.

She began telling me I was "the man of the family," and insisting that I play the role. She took me to a Newark department store and bought me a suit with knickers, a herringbone pattern that must have represented a large fortune on her meager resources. But a suit and a necktie and a white shirt weren't enough; she also insisted on buying me a hat, a junior-scale model of the gray fedora Uncle Allen wore.

"You're the man of the family now," she said. "You have to dress like a gentleman."

The suit and hat were only for special occasions, of course. Like church. Men who wanted to make something of themselves went to church, and they went well dressed. Each Sunday she rolled me off the couch to put on the suit and accompany her to the Wesley Methodist Church on Washington Avenue. Her "Papa" had been a Methodist, and he had been a good man. She would start me out as a Methodist, and never mind that my father and all his people had always been Lutherans.

On the journey to church she instructed me in how a proper man must walk with a woman. "A gentleman always walks on the outside," she explained, maneuvering me to the curb edge on the sidewalk. If in childish excitement I dashed ahead of her and ran through a door she called me back for another lesson in manhood: "The man always opens the door for a woman and holds it so she can go first." . . .

It was at this time that my mother decided to acquaint me with work and obtained my job selling the *Saturday Evening Post*. In typical weeks my magazine sales earned me twenty-five to thirty-five cents. She took a dime of this to deposit in a bank account she had opened for me. "A man has to get in the habit of saving for a rainy day." As "the man of the family," I was expected to contribute another nickel in support of the household. The remaining ten or twenty cents was mine to squan-

[1]Doris: Baker's sister.

der on vices of my choice, which were movies, Big Little Books, and two-for-a-penny Mary Jane bars.

The making of a man, even when the raw material was as pliable as I, often seemed brutally hard without the help of a father to handle the rougher passages. There was the awkward problem of punishment. Small, not prepossessing, certainly not strong, she was wedded to the old saw "Spare the rod and spoil the child" and feared that unless my misbehaviors were corrected with corporal punishment my character would become soft and corrupt.

Before declaring me "the man of the family" she had never spanked me, and by that time, when I was eight, I was too large for spanking. It was her notion, picked up I know not where, that boys my age needed "a good thrashing" when they misbehaved. These she administered with my belt, often for what seemed to me like trivial offenses such as coming home late for supper because I was having a good time sledding on the hill. A man had a responsibility to meet his social obligations on time. Small as she was, she could still make the snapping belt sting when it lashed across my bared legs, but I hated the indignity of these beatings so much that I refused to satisfy her with a discreetly faked show of tears.

I had no real tears in me at that time. I hadn't cried since my father's death, not even on the day . . . when my mother called me into the house and said, "I've got something to tell you now, and I don't want you to cry," and told me my grandmother had died in Morrisonville. In spite of my mother's words I knew I was expected to cry for Ida Rebecca, but I couldn't and didn't even want to. If in playing I tore my knee on a nail or one of the boys straddled me on the ground and pounded my face with fists until I was spitting blood, I did not cry because of the pain. I found myself thinking, "This hurts"; or if I was being beaten in a fight, I stared at my assailant in silent rage, thinking, "Some day I'll get you back for this," and when it was over limped homeward dry of eye, holding a bloody nose.

My failure to cry during her "thrashings" enraged my mother, and I knew it. Tears would be evidence that I had learned the lesson. My sullen submission to her heaviest blows intensified her fury. If she had been a man she would have been able to make me weep for mercy, but because she was not, and because I did not weep, she struck all the harder.

I knew that faking the tears would gratify her and end the punishment, but I refused. The injustice and humiliation of being beaten rankled so powerfully that I deliberately accepted the worst she could deliver to show my contempt. Sometimes, to goad her with proof of my contempt, I gritted my teeth and, when the belt had fallen four or five times, muttered, "That doesn't hurt me." In these moments we were very close to raw hatred of each other. We were two wills of iron. She was determined to break me; I was just as determined that she would not.

In the end she was the one who always cried, and then, when she had flung the belt aside and collapsed on a chair weeping quietly, the anger and hatred instantly drained out of me, and overcome with pity and love, I rushed to embrace and kiss her, saying, "It's all right, Mama, it's all right. I'll never do it again. I promise, I'll never do it again."

Response and Analysis

1. Russell Baker says that the expectations held for him were different from those held for his sister. He claims that his sister "was not expected to take up the heavy burdens" that he was expected to assume. To what burdens does he refer? Today, girls and boys socialized differently for their eventual adult roles? Support your view by giving a few examples of how boys and girls are socialized.

2. Baker believes that his mother's determination to make a man out of him was a way of redeeming her failed youth and proving the strength of her womanhood. Is it common for parents to attempt to live out their aspirations and longings through their children? Why or why not? What are the costs and benefits of parents treating their children in this way?

3. In trying to secure compliance from her son, Mrs. Baker uses physical punishment. According to Baker, what is his mother's attitude toward spanking and her probable motivation for administering it? What is Baker's reaction to the punishment? How does spanking affect him? Do you think that spanking should ever be used as a disciplinary strategy in raising children? Why or why not?

Research

Suppose you want to examine why some children, but not others, are able to bounce back emotionally and psychologically after losing a parent at a young age. You decide to focus on a trait labeled *resilience*—an inner strength that allows children and adults to successfully cope with and overcome the challenges they face. You want to know how the personalities of resilient children differ from those of less-resilient children. To address this question, you will need to identify children who are resilient and children who are not so resilient. What individual differences (for instance, temperament, intelligence, cognitive habits, social skills) do you expect to be associated with resilience? Why? What social and environmental variables may be associated with resilience? Why? State your predictions as hypotheses.

SIBLING RIVALRY, SIBLING LOVE

Nancy Samalin with Catherine Whitney

Developmental Concepts
children's adjustment to a new sibling, sibling conflict,
family relationships

Author and parenting specialist Nancy Samalin describes sibling rivalry as inevitable and not necessarily harmful. Samalin understands the fears and feelings of children who learn that the baby just brought from the hospital is home to stay. As children grow, the competition begins, and, by middle childhood, brothers and sisters have ready complaints against each other. In this selection, we may detect mischievous delight in their accusations, but we may hear sibling pride and allegiance as well. Although their complaints are genuine, most siblings learn to tolerate, appreciate, enjoy, and love one another.

Except for twins, every firstborn or first-adopted child is an *only* child for a time. The experience of parenting the first is unique, scary, precious—a new and dramatic adventure. It is the transformation from an adult-centered to a child-centered household. Many parents believe that once they have made the transition from having no children to having their first, the rest should be smooth sailing. But the arrival of a second child is a disruption with unique features all its own. Even after elaborate preparation, the introduction of a sibling can be a frustrating process— especially for your first child. After all, a young child who hears, "We're having another child because we love you so much," is not warmed by such a sentiment. To his way of thinking it's not that different from a husband who says to his wife, "I love you so much and I'm so happy with you that I want to double my joy. So I'm getting another wife. She may be a little younger and cuter, but you can share me, as well as all your favorite things, with her!"

Eric was only one year old when I brought Todd home from the hospital. To this day, I remember the scene. When I went to hug Eric, he stiffened and turned his face away from me. I was shocked by his reaction. I didn't see things through his eyes: Not only had I left him for a few days but I returned with someone else! He was not about to agree that we were doing something wonderful for him by presenting him with a baby brother. At the time, I couldn't understand how different this "blessed event" appeared from his perspective.

Kids are concrete thinkers. They see love as something to be measured out. They don't realize that the more you have, the more you have to give. To them, love is as finite as M&M's; if you give some away, there won't be as much left for them. So when a new baby is vying for your attention, they're likely to see the baby as an unwelcome interloper.

I doubt if there's an only child in existence who isn't shocked when his or her solitary reign ends. I love the story that the writer Anna Quindlen tells about how this realization dawned on her firstborn child when he wanted her attention and she couldn't oblige. She writes: "It began one day when the younger one needed me more, and I turned to my older son, Quin, and said, 'You know, Quin, I'm Christopher's mommy, too.' The look that passed over his face was the one that usually accompanies the discovery of a dead body in the den: shock, denial, horror. 'And Daddy is Christopher's daddy, too?' he gasped. When I confirmed this, he began to cry—wet, sad sobbing."

When I ask parents why they decided to have more than one child, the most common answer is that they did it for the sake of their first child—to give him or her the "gift" of a sibling. I often hear adults who were only children themselves talking about how lonely it was to grow up without brothers and sisters, and how much they longed for a sibling. They are convinced that it will mean a lot to their own children to have sibling companions.

But parents are almost always shocked when the "gift" isn't welcome—when their children act more like enemies than friends, when the bickering and jealousy and rivalry are constants rather than the loving companionship they had hoped for.

One of my favorite stories about sibling rivalry was told by the writer Louise Bates Ames, a child development expert from the Gesell Institute. She described a woman who was pregnant with her second child. One day, her three-year-old son kept poking her belly harder and harder. While restraining him, she thought to ask, "Are you trying to say something to the baby?"

"Yeah," he replied. "Come on out and fight."

We don't like it, but sibling battles are a fact of life. It is one of the more upsetting aspects of parenting to see your kids bickering and being antagonistic toward one another. But if it is the nature of adults to long for peace, it is the nature of children to upset domestic tranquillity.

Kids Fight over the Darnedest Things

What do siblings fight about? The short answer is everything and nothing. Parents I've interviewed on the subject frequently used the words "silly things" when asked what their children fought about. These included: who sits where (at home and in the car), what TV programs to watch, who holds the remote control, who gets to choose the snack, who plays with which toy, who picks the movie, who turns on the light, who gets to lie on Mommy's pillow, which one gets into the car first—as well as squabbles over real and imagined inequities. It drives parents crazy!

The parents I surveyed had plenty to say about why their kids fight. Many of their comments will probably sound familiar:

- "Fairness in a zillion forms—size and number of toys, number of play dates in a week, length of school day, and so on. My six-year-old is obsessed with everything being equal with the four-year-old."
- "Often, I never know what they're fighting about. One of them will just come indoors saying, 'He pushed me.' Or 'She made a face at me.' Or 'He's bothering me.' The other day I had to laugh. It was, 'She breathed on me!'"
- "Everything! If they don't have something specific to fight about, they just tease and harass each other. Like last night, they were arguing about whose blue coat was bluer!"
- "My son says the only time he fights with his older sister is when she won't play with him. He has a limitless passion for playing games and make-believe with her, and she, as the older one, gets bored. So, typically, she will shut him out of her room and he will rage and mope."
- "Who gets to turn off the television. Who gets to turn on the light. Who gets to stand on the stool at the bathroom sink. Also, they fight when one splashes the other in the bathtub, when one hurts the other, when one won't play a game that the other wants to play, or when they both want to play the same game—alone!"
- "Stupid things! Any little scrap of paper that one picks up, the other will suddenly covet it. 'He's sitting in my chair.' 'How come she's not picking up when I have to?' 'I wanted to open the front door.' I'm convinced they mostly fight to get my attention, and they do get it since it's so hard to ignore their squabbling."

One mother told me that her children used to argue loudly and passionately about the temperature at which water boiled in the mountains. "They fought about it so frequently that it became a family joke. The question never got resolved, so I decided that they just liked to fight about it."

The fact is, kids fight about anything and everything simply because it's the fighting itself, not its content, that holds endless appeal. Parents forget that fighting can be fun, and it's never boring. They worry that sibling fights are a grim precursor to a lifetime of hatred. Sometimes they can't believe these are really their children. "I'm always thinking, I'm not supposed to have these kids," said Zoe, a gentle, soft-spoken young mother of two very aggressive boys. "How can these be my kids? I'm such a pacifist, and I hate noise and disorder. I half believe my boys came from the cabbage patch—or, more likely, the planet Jupiter!"

Last year, I had an opportunity to conduct a workshop for young people at the Hudson School in Hoboken, New Jersey. Over the years, I've listened to thousands of parents tell me what it was like to raise more than one child, so I was eager to hear the kids themselves discuss their feelings about having siblings.

I arrived at the Hudson School not quite knowing what to expect. The principal, Suellen Newman, had assembled a group of boys and girls between the ages of nine and sixteen. All of them had brothers and sisters, and naturally they were glad to be called out of their regular classes to participate. But I felt a bit of trepidation. Frankly, I anticipated that our time together would deteriorate into a gripe session.

Not surprisingly, there was plenty of that. But I was also delightfully surprised to discover among these children a deep reservoir of pleasure at having siblings. I had the sense that even when they were describing the things that annoyed or angered them, there was an underlying acceptance of this being just the way it was supposed to be.

They really enjoyed our time together, and seemed to have fun venting and griping—but with a fundamental affection and warmth that was unmistakable in their smiles and enthusiasm. This dialogue was typical:

Ashley: I have two brothers. One is seven and one is five and a half. They're monsters.

Me: They're monsters? Oh. Anyone else have monster siblings?

Tamelah: Oh, yes!

Lori: Their socks smell.

Jeffrey: Thanks. Thanks a lot. My socks do not smell.

This dialogue was followed by uproarious laughter. Nilmarie, nine, added, "My brother is sixteen and he treats me like a baby. He calls me shrimp and I hate that. And he's always torturing me."

"What does he do?" I asked Nilmarie.

"Well," she said, "like there's this huge sofa and everybody in the house loves sitting on the sofa. So when my brother sits on the sofa, I say, 'Mom wants you in the kitchen.' So he goes to the kitchen and I stretch out on the sofa. Then he comes back and throws me on the floor."

"I don't blame him!" I said.

"You think that's bad?" Anna, ten, interrupted eagerly. "I don't think so. My big brother does worse things, like holding me upside down until my face turns blue. He's eighteen. I'm telling you, big brothers are trouble."

The group launched into a passionate tirade against older brothers, younger brothers, older sisters, and younger sisters—vying for the position of most tormented. I sat back and noticed how much they were enjoying themselves. I got a kick out of watching their animated faces and the enthusiasm with which they launched into their complaints, each one wanting to outdo the others. Here was an enjoyable opportunity to vent that they probably didn't get at home.

I also noticed that their gripes were pretty mundane. There was little evidence of true, abiding hatred. In fact, moments after Anna proclaimed her eighteen-year-old brother to be the worst of all, she said, "Last month we took him to college, and I just had to go back into the car because I was crying. Because he was going to stay there for five months."

"You were really going to miss him," I said.

Anna nodded her head in wonder. "I was sobbing. I couldn't believe it. I mean, that's the brother that I fight with the most, that I kick, who beats me up. And there I am crying."

"Does that seem crazy to you?" I asked Anna. She shrugged. "No, because sometimes I like to tease him and it's fun when he teases me."

Several of the kids commented that older siblings were a piece of cake compared to younger siblings. Often, the complaint was that the younger ones got away with murder. Michael, eleven, was frustrated because his four-year-old sister seemed to get all the breaks while he got all the blame. I asked him for an example.

"Okay," he said. "She'll be lying on the bed and she'll fall off. And she goes and cries to our mom, 'Michael pushed me off the bed.'"

"Why do you think she does that?" I asked.

"She doesn't want to admit she's clumsy. So she blames me."

"What does your mother say?" I asked.

"Mom comes in and goes, 'Why did you push your sister?' and I'm like, 'No, I didn't.' But she believes my sister. Then I get punished, like I can't watch TV for a while."

"That must get you pretty mad," I said sympathetically.

Michael smirked. "Yeah. I get back at her, though. Like, when we play, I trip her occasionally." His reply produced giggles from the group. Kids appreciate the justice of reciprocity.

We talked for an hour, each child delighting in his or her complaints about siblings. But as our time together drew to a close, I asked the kids if there were good things about having siblings. Everyone agreed that having more than one child was best. "I had a friend who was an only child," Alex said. "And he was pampered beyond belief. He had nothing to do when he was at home. At least when I get home, there's brothers and sisters to scream at. I'm like deaf when my brother is blasting his stereo beyond all hell." And that seemed to sum things up perfectly. . . .

As the children at Hudson School demonstrated, kids are capable of moving easily between complaint and appreciation in the blink of an eye. While parents torture themselves with the horrible things their children say and do to one another, and imagine them growing up as lifelong enemies, the children themselves are often having the time of their lives bickering and plotting and, finally, loving each other.

Children can help parents lighten up and let go of their guilt. For example, the children I've talked to are almost unanimous in their belief that it is better to have siblings than to be only children—in spite (and even because) of the fighting, competition, and the reluctant sharing. In their refreshing way, kids are able to take things in stride that make their parents' hair stand on end. And that's a great lesson for the harried parent.

Response and Analysis

1. Why do children feel threatened by the arrival of a new baby in the family? In what ways are their fears and feelings based in reality, that is, on real threats? In what ways are their feelings unrealistic? What can parents do to help first-born children feel more comfortable with a new sibling?

2. What are the psychological benefits for an older sibling in having a younger brother or sister? What are the benefits for the younger sibling? What are the psychological risks for the older sibling? For the younger sibling? Is there an ideal age difference that is beneficial for siblings to have a close relationship? Why or why not?

3. According to Nancy Samalin, siblings fight over many seemingly trivial issues. What are some of the reasons that siblings quarrel? What does Samalin suggest parents could learn from siblings' quarrels?

Research

Suppose you hypothesize that children with siblings have more opportunity for peer-oriented social interaction than do only children. As a result, you suspect that children with siblings develop social skills faster than do only children. You decide to compare the social skills of six- to ten-year-old children who have siblings with those who do not have siblings. After obtaining approval from the Institutional Review Board at your college or university, the cooperation of the school, and the informed consent of the children's parents, you are ready to begin.

You will identify two groups of children—those with siblings and those without—who are alike in most other respects, and have them take part in a structured activity that allows for social interaction. Design an activity so children who have siblings interact with children who do not have siblings. What activity would you use to elicit the social interaction? Why? You videotape the children's sessions and then ask your research assistants, who do not know the purpose of the study, to rate each child's social behaviors and social skills. Why is it important that the research assistants do not know the purpose of the study? If each videotape is reviewed by only one research assistant, is it possible that one assistant might "see" and record behaviors that another assistant might not see or record? How could you increase the reliability of this procedure?

A BILINGUAL CHILDHOOD

Richard Rodriguez

Developmental Concept
bilingualism: cognitive and social effects

What are the challenges for a child who goes to school not speaking the language of the land? Richard Rodriguez grew up in a Spanish-speaking section of Sacramento, California, and was caught between two cultures: that of his family and that of the culture outside of his home. The nuns of his school strongly urged that Richard learn English and that the family speak English in their home. This was not easy for the parents, but wanting their children to succeed, they consented. Once he began using English, Rodriguez's life with his parents and his intimate, protected world of home and neighborhood changed. What does the boy gain and what does he lose by adopting a new language?

I remember, to start with, that day in Sacramento, in a California now nearly thirty years past, when I first entered a classroom—able to understand about fifty stray English words. The third of four children, I had been preceded by my older brother and sister to a neighborhood Roman Catholic school. But neither of them had revealed very much about their classroom experiences. . . .

Because I wrongly imagined that English was intrinsically a public language and Spanish was intrinsically private, I easily noted the difference between classroom language and the language at home. At school, words were directed to a general audience of listeners. ("Boys and girls . . .") Words were meaningfully ordered. And the point was not self-expression alone, but to make oneself understood by many others. The teacher quizzed: "Boys and girls, why do we use that word in this sentence? Could we think of a better word to use there? Would the sentence change its meaning if the words were differently arranged? Isn't there a better way of saying much the same thing?" (I couldn't say. I wouldn't try to say.)

Three months passed. Five. A half year. Unsmiling, ever watchful, my teachers noted my silence. They began to connect my behavior with the slow progress my brother and sisters were making. Until, one Saturday morning, three nuns arrived at the house to talk to our parents. Stiffly they sat on the blue living room sofa. From the doorway of another room, spying on the visitors, I noted the incongruity, the clash of two worlds, the faces and voices of school intruding upon the familiar setting of home. I overheard one voice gently wondering, "Do your children speak only Spanish at home, Mrs. Rodriguez?" While another voice added, "That Richard especially seems so timid and shy."

That Rich-heard!

With great tact, the visitors continued, "Is it possible for you and your husband to encourage your children to practice their English when they are home?" Of course my parents complied. What would they not do for their children's wellbeing? And how could they question the Church's authority which those women represented? In an instant they agreed to give up the language (the sounds) which had revealed and accentuated our family's closeness. The moment after the visitors left, the change was observed. "*Ahora*, speak to us only *en inglés*," my father and mother told us.

At first, it seemed a kind of game. After dinner each night, the family gathered together to practice "our" English. It was still *inglés*, a language foreign to us, so we felt drawn to it as strangers. Laughing, we would try to define words we could not pronounce. We played with strange English sounds, often overanglicizing our pronunciations. And we filled the smiling gaps of our sentences with familiar Spanish sounds. But that was cheating, somebody shouted, and everyone laughed.

In school, meanwhile, like my brother and sisters, I was required to attend a daily tutoring session. I needed a full year of this special work. I also needed my teachers to keep my attention from straying in class by calling out, "*Rich-heard*"— their English voices slowly loosening the ties to my other name, with its three notes, *Ri-car-do*. Most of all, I needed to hear my mother and father speak to me in a moment of seriousness in "broken"—suddenly heartbreaking—English. This scene was inevitable. One Saturday morning I entered the kitchen where my parents were talking, but I did not realize that they were talking in Spanish until, the moment they saw me, their voices changed and they began speaking English. The gringo sounds they uttered startled me. Pushed me away. In that moment of trivial misunderstanding and profound insight, I felt my throat twisted by unsounded grief. I simply turned and left the room. But I had no place to escape to where I could grieve in Spanish. My brother and sisters were speaking English in another part of the house.

Again and again in the days following, as I grew increasingly angry, I was obliged to hear my mother and father encouraging me: "Speak to us *en inglés*." Only then did I determine to learn classroom English. Thus, sometime afterward it happened: One day in school, I raised my hand to volunteer an answer to a question. I spoke out in a loud voice and I did not think it remarkable when the entire class understood. That day I moved very far from being the disadvantaged child I had been only days earlier. Taken hold at last was the belief, the calming assurance, that I *belonged* in public.

Shortly after, I stopped hearing the high, troubling sounds of *los gringos*. A more and more confident speaker of English, I didn't listen to how strangers sounded when they talked to me. With so many English-speaking people around me, I no longer heard American accents. Conversations quickened. Listening to persons whose voices sounded eccentrically pitched, I might note their sounds for a few seconds, but then I'd concentrate on what they were saying. Now when I heard someone's tone of voice—angry or questioning or sarcastic or happy or sad—I didn't distinguish it from the words it expressed. Sound and word were thus tightly wedded. At the end of each day I was often bemused, and always relieved, to realize how "soundless," though crowded with words, my day in public had been. An eight-year-old boy, I finally came to accept what had been technically true since my birth: I was an American citizen.

But diminished by then was the special feeling of closeness at home. Gone was the desperate, urgent, intense feeling of being at home among those with whom I felt intimate. Our family remained a loving family, but one greatly changed. We were no longer so close, no longer bound tightly together by the knowledge of our separateness from *los gringos*. Neither my older brother nor my sisters rushed home after school any more. Nor did I. When I arrived home, often there would be neighborhood kids in the house. Or the house would be empty of sounds.

Following the dramatic Americanization of their children, even my parents grew more publicly confident—especially my mother. First she learned the names of all the people on the block. Then she decided we needed to have a telephone in our house. My father, for his part, continued to use the word *gringo*, but it was no longer charged with bitterness or distrust. Stripped of any emotional content, the word simply became a name for those Americans not of Hispanic descent. Hearing him, sometimes, I wasn't sure if he was pronouncing the Spanish word *gringo*, or saying gringo in English.

There was a new silence at home. As we children learned more and more English, we shared fewer and fewer words with our parents. Sentences needed to be spoken slowly when one of us addressed our mother or father. Often the parent wouldn't understand. The child would need to repeat himself. Still the parent misunderstood. The young voice, frustrated, would end up saying, "Never mind"—the subject was closed. Dinners would be noisy with the clinking of knives and forks against dishes. My mother would smile softly between her remarks; my father, at the other end of the table, would chew and chew his food while he stared over the heads of his children.

My mother! My father! After English became my primary language, I no longer knew what words to use in addressing my parents. The old Spanish words (those tender accents of sound) I had earlier used—*mamá* and *papá*—I couldn't use any more. They would have been all-too-painful reminders of how much had changed in my life. On the other hand, the words I heard neighborhood kids call their parents seemed equally unsatisfactory. "Mother" and "father," "ma," "papa," "pa," "dad," "pop" (how I hated the all-American sound of that last word)—all these I felt were unsuitable terms of address for *my* parents. As a result, I never used them at home. Whenever I'd speak to my parents, I would try to get their attention by looking at them. In public conversations, I'd refer to them as my "parents" or my "mother" and "father."

My mother and father, for their part, responded differently, as their children spoke to them less. My mother grew restless, seemed troubled and anxious at the scarceness of words exchanged in the house. She would question me about my day when I came home from school. She smiled at my small talk. She pried at the edges of my sentences to get me to say something more. ("What . . .?") She'd join conversations she overheard, but her intrusions often stopped her children's talking. By contrast, my father seemed to grow reconciled to the new quiet. Though his English somewhat improved, he tended more and more to retire into silence. At dinner he spoke very little. One night his children and even his wife helplessly giggled at his garbled English pronunciation of the Catholic "Grace Before Meals." Thereafter he made his wife recite the prayer at the start of each meal, even on formal occasions when there were guests in the house.

Hers became the public voice of the family. On official business it was she, not my father, who would usually talk to strangers on the phone or in stores. We children grew so accustomed to his silence that years later we would routinely refer to his "shyness." (My mother often tried to explain: Both of his parents died when he was eight. He was raised by an uncle who treated him as little more than a menial servant. He was never encouraged to speak. He grew up alone—a man of few words.) But I realized my father was not shy whenever I'd watch him speaking Spanish with relatives. Using Spanish, he was quickly effusive. Especially when talking with other men, his voice would spark, flicker, flare alive with varied sounds. In Spanish he expressed ideas and feelings he rarely revealed when speaking English. With firm Spanish sounds he conveyed a confidence and authority that English would never allow him.

The silence at home, however, was not simply the result of fewer words passing between parents and children. More profound for me was the silence created by my inattention to sounds. At about the time I no longer bothered to listen with care to the sounds of English in public, I grew careless about listening to the sounds made by the family when they spoke. Most of the time I would hear someone speaking at home and didn't distinguish his sounds from the words people uttered in public. I didn't even pay much attention to my parents' accented and ungrammatical speech—at least not at home. Only when I was with them in public would I become alert to their accents. But even then their sounds caused me less and less concern. For I was growing increasingly confident of my own public identity.

I would have been happier about my public success had I not recalled, sometimes, what it had been like earlier, when my family conveyed its intimacy through a set of conveniently private sounds. Sometimes in public, hearing a stranger, I'd hark back to my lost past. A Mexican farm worker approached me one day downtown. He wanted directions to some place. "*Hijito,* . . ." he said. And his voice stirred old longings. Another time I was standing beside my mother in the visiting room of a Carmelite convent, before the dense screen which rendered the nuns shadowy figures. I heard several of them speaking Spanish in their busy, singsong, overlapping voices, assuring my mother that, yes, yes, we were remembered, all our family was remembered, in their prayers. Those voices echoed faraway family sounds. Another day a dark-faced old woman touched my shoulder lightly to steady herself as she boarded a bus. She murmured something to me I couldn't quite comprehend. Her Spanish voice came near, like the face of a never-before-seen relative in the instant before I was kissed. That voice, like so many of the Spanish voices I'd hear in public, recalled the golden age of my childhood.

Response and Analysis

1. How did not knowing English affect Richard Rodriguez's schoolwork, his social life, and his life with his family? How did his learning English change his life as he was growing up?

2. Psychologist Walter Lambert distinguishes between additive and subtractive bilingualism. With additive bilingualism, an individual respects both the native language and the secondary language and is proficient in both. With subtractive bilingualism, an individual becomes proficient in the new, second language and loses proficiency in the first language; eventually, the second language replaces the first. As Rodriguez became more proficient in English, would you expect that he would become more or less proficient in Spanish? Why?

3. Some children learn to speak two languages at the same time. How might learning two languages simultaneously influence the cognitive development of young children?

4. More than six million children in the United States come from homes in which English is not the native language. It is estimated that the number of bilingual children will triple in the twenty-first century. Suppose your local school board is developing a new policy on how to instruct elementary school children who are not proficient in English. The board members tell you that, in some schools in the district, as many as twenty

different languages are spoken by the student body as a whole. They ask you to offer a few recommendations on how to instruct non-English-speaking students. List five recommendations and explain why each would be effective.

Research

Suppose you want to conduct a study to compare the intelligence of bilingual and monolingual children. When choosing children to participate in your study, you make sure that you have an equal number of bilingual and monolingual boys and girls of the same age, that they have about the same number of brothers and sisters, and that they have lived in the United States for approximately the same number of years. Unfortunately, you have difficulty matching the participants on socioeconomic status: most of the bilingual children live in upper-class neighborhoods and most of the monolingual children live in lower-class neighborhoods. After securing the approval of the Institutional Review Board at your college or university and permission from the children's parents, you administer an intelligence test to each student. You find that bilingual children have higher intelligence test scores than monolingual children. Can you conclude that bilingualism is beneficial? Why or why not? What other factors may have influenced the relationship between bilingualism and intelligence test scores? If you were to repeat this study, what changes would you make to minimize these problems?

THE SPATIAL CHILD

John Philo Dixon

Developmental Concepts
special abilities, learning to read, motivation

John Philo Dixon, now the research director for the American Shakespeare Theater, recalls how not being a good reader made him feel inadequate. His first-grade teacher threatened to hold him back from second grade and children teased him about his reading ability. These experiences had a negative effect on his self-esteem. Although he became more comfortable with reading in later years, he had few academic successes during his elementary and middle school years. Finally, in ninth grade, Dixon realized that he had a special talent for math—a talent that for too long had gone unrecognized. To what extent did motivation and desire influence Dixon's ultimate achievements in school? How do various approaches to intelligence recognize special abilities in children?

It was a combination of mystification and depression that set in when Mrs. Wilson struggled at introducing me to reading in the first grade. As I looked around at my classmates, their ease at turning written words into the correct spoken words seemed to make them coconspirators. They possessed a secret wisdom to which I was not privy. Mrs. Wilson looked upon them with eyes of pleasure. They were her teacher's delight, her measure of success. She looked upon me with eyes of forlorn patience. I was the stumbling block in her attempt to deliver a class full of readers to the second grade teachers. I remember sitting bent low at my school desk, eyes downward, hoping not to be noticed as I bumbled over *Dick and Jane*.

Panic struck me when my mother had to visit school to talk about my difficulties. My mother had never had doubts about me. I could run, I could talk, I could play games, I could build things, I could sing—all those things that mark normalcy to a hopeful mother. Mrs. Wilson had found me defective, and I had become a problem child, even to those who were most dear to me. My mother's visit to Mrs. Wilson also caused terror in the confusion of my child's mind. I feared that my unused schemes to cheat on spelling tests—a strategic planning undertaken in the desire to avoid being lowest in the class—might have been found out. Perhaps Mrs. Wilson in her infinite wisdom could even read into the hearts of little boys. However, the conference had only to do with my incompetence. My mother sat beside Mrs. Wilson, and I sat at my desk across the otherwise empty room. My ears strained to hear bits and pieces of the litany of my problems. Mrs. Wilson concluded that I wasn't prepared to go on to second grade. Flunking was the ultimate stigma for a school child in rural Nebraska. It would have put my self-regard at the lowest of levels. To my everlasting gratitude, things weren't left at that. A deal was struck between Mrs. Wilson and my mother. I would only be allowed to enter second grade in the fall if my mother gave me special instruction in reading for the whole summer vacation. My mother's reading lessons had little more effect than those of Mrs. Wilson. I tried, but reading wasn't yet in me.

I entered second grade as much a nonreader as before, but thanked my lucky stars that I had made it, and braced for another year of being the uninformed outsider in a society of secret code decipherers. Sometime during the second grade I began to catch on to reading, and I don't remember being in serious threat of flunking after that. My school performance settled into the slow-poke category for most of elementary school. There were a few breaks in this eight-year stint of questionable reputation. There was the day the second grade teacher asked several students to make a line a yard long on the chalkboard without looking at the yard stick. Mine came closest to being the right length. The teacher hardly noticed this insignificant victory of one of her more unpromising students, but for me it was one of those rare triumphs that stands etched in my mind.

My third grade teacher told my mother there was a lot going on in my mind. How did she guess? In the small town in which I grew up, the "farmerish" wisdom of silence would occasionally be applied to me; more than a few times people would take note of my basically unspoken character and say, "Still water runs deep." I never did know how to take that. Was deep good or bad?

There was the week in Miss Reine's fourth grade class. I was allowed to help construct a model colonial village. I made houses, a stockade, and an intricate little spinning wheel. It was the most glorious week in elementary school. As far as I was concerned, it could have gone on forever. However, then it was necessary to move on to the "real" work of school. Miss Reine told me that I couldn't work on the model any more because I had spent too much time and gotten behind in my school work.

Throughout these eight years there was an interesting discrepancy. Although my reading never changed from a slow to halting pace, I nevertheless loved reading. Sometimes I would spend every minute possible devouring whole sets of books from the library bookcase in the back of the classroom; slowly, ruminatingly, but devouring. There was no way my reading could be rushed. Deep twinges of anguish accompanied speed reading drills. I would pretend to be reading faster than I could because I didn't want to be the last student to raise his hand to indicate being finished. Most of all I hated reading tests. If I didn't rush through tests much faster than I could possibly comprehend the material, I would find myself far from the end of the test when the time was called. Yet there were times when I spent all the time I could reading. Books were the entry way to the larger world. The ideas in books were marvelous even if my reading mechanics were tortuous. The ideas in books came to be an important focus of my life, and I would learn to put up with the difficulty for the sake of learning.

Crude drawing was something I did through my childhood, even though I don't remember ever having an art class or being encouraged in any way. In the early grades I would draw what I thought of as the structures of buildings; the beam patterns of skyscrapers and things like that. I was sort of embarrassed for doing these sketches because I didn't know why I wanted to. . . . I just did. Later I took up making crude architectural plans for buildings. I enjoyed music, sang in the chorus, and played different instruments in the band. Music was in me, and if I weren't so shy, I might have been a good musical performer, although I never learned to read music very well.

When I entered algebra class in the ninth grade, the long depression of elementary school ended. Algebra was fascinating to me from the moment I encountered it. In algebra I was the best in my class, and it wasn't just a momentary triumph like when I drew the most accurate length of a yard stick in second grade. My triumph in algebra stuck. In geometry and physics, I was even better. For the physics class in eleventh grade my school was participating in a statewide experiment to see whether instruction through a set of movies was better than regular instruction. My school had regular instruction and my teacher, Mr. Kasle, was good. As a part of the experiment, every other week we would take a special test, which would be sent to a university for scoring. When the scores came back, I would be several points above anyone else in the class. Having lived through the nightmare of the elementary school, I savored every moment of these victories, but savored them in trepidation that they were somehow a fluke, in fear that my incompetencies would descend upon me and I would once again fail. I live in fear of that to this day. It is not easy to free oneself of eight years of degradation when it is experienced at an age too young to have had a chance to know that success is also possible.

Sometime in the ninth grade my class was given a nonverbal IQ test. I don't know exactly how I scored on this test, but there were hints that I had done very well, and after the testing, I was accorded much more respect by my school teachers than before. Had the IQ test been a verbal one, the results, of course, would have been entirely opposite and I would have been seen as anything but brilliant.

There was no program for gifted children in the high school, but the teachers seemed to sense my need and arranged for me to take a correspondence course in advanced algebra. I received a text book in the mail along with my first assignment. I would do my assignments, send them off to the university, and receive them back corrected along with the next assignment. This solitary exercise in doing lists of algebra problems for a disembodied tutor did little to spark my imagination. Though I appreciate the good intention on my behalf in making this arrangement, I would most likely have been better off spending some extra time with Mr. Kasle, the local science teacher who seemed to have a good scientific mind.

The discrepancies in my abilities have persisted. When I took the Graduate Record Exam (GRE) at the completion of undergraduate school, my mathematics score was in the top 2 percent, while my verbal score was just barely in the top quarter. This difference has continually resulted in what to others may seem like an uneven performance. To the extent that tasks depend on a careful understanding of the spatial-mechanical world around me, I usually do quite well. To the extent that it depends on quick verbal analysis, my performance can seem debilitated.

As a child I thought of my problem as personal, and I endured it in silence. Now I cannot be so generous. I see no reason that children who have considerable ability of a distinct kind should be taught that they are inadequate, if not stupid.

Response and Analysis

1. Given John Philo Dixon's difficulties in learning how to read, how does he come to enjoy reading? How do his experiences with reading affect his self-esteem? How does the validation of his mathematical and spatial ability affect his self-esteem?

2. What does Dixon's score on the Graduate Record Exam suggest about his verbal and quantitative abilities? Why does he fear that his success with mathematics and physics may be a "fluke"?

3. What types of learning experiences might cause some children in elementary and secondary school to develop low self-esteem? How might these experiences affect an individual's sense of self when he or she becomes an adult? What might a teacher do to minimize these negative experiences? To pro- mote positive experiences that may enhance self-esteem?

4. How does Dixon's experience relate to theories of intelligence proposed by Howard Gardner? By Robert Sternberg?

Research

Suppose you want to know whether a child's performance on an intelligence test is influenced by the gender of the test administrator. You hypothesize that children will score higher when the test is administered by someone of the same gender than by someone of the opposite gender. Imagine that you conduct the study and find that the children's scores are the same regardless of the test administrator's gender. Based on this finding, would you accept or reject the null hypothesis? Why or why not?

HANDED MY OWN LIFE

Annie Dillard

Developmental Concepts
industry, achievement, intrinsic motivation, extrinsic
motivation, sense of self, curiosity

One Christmas, Annie Dillard's parents give her what she had longed for: a
microscope. By spring, she is able to gather some puddle water that she hopes will
yield an amoeba for her to see. Placing the drop of water on the slide under the
lens, Dillard is elated: "I would have known him anywhere," she writes, "blobby
and grainy as his picture." Excited, she runs to her parents. They must come and
see her find. But they tell her that they are content with what they are doing and do
not need to come with her right then. Why don't they go with her? What gift did her
parents give her by not coming to share in her find?

After I read *The Field Book of Ponds and Streams* several times, I longed for a microscope. Everybody needed a microscope. Detectives used microscopes, both for
the FBI and at Scotland Yard. Although usually I had to save my tiny allowance for
things I wanted, that year for Christmas my parents gave me a microscope kit.

In a dark basement corner, on a white enamel table, I set up the microscope
kit. I supplied a chair, a lamp, a batch of jars, a candle, and a pile of library books.
The microscope kit supplied a blunt black three-speed microscope, a booklet, a scalpel, a dropper, an ingenious device for cutting thin segments of fragile tissue, a pile
of clean slides and cover slips, and a dandy array of corked test tubes.

One of the test tubes contained "hay infusion." Hay infusion was a wee brown
chip of grass blade. You added water to it, and after a week it became a jungle in a
drop, full of one-celled animals. This did not work for me. All I saw in the microscope after a week was a wet chip of dried grass, much enlarged.

Another test tube contained "diatomaceous earth." This was, I believed, an actual pinch of the white cliffs of Dover. On my palm it was an airy, friable chalk. The
booklet said it was composed of the silicaceous bodies of diatoms—one-celled creatures that lived in, as it were, small glass jewelry boxes with fitted lids. Diatoms, I
read, come in a variety of transparent geometrical shapes. Broken and dead and dug
out of geological deposits, they made chalk, and a fine abrasive used in silver polish
and toothpaste. What I saw in the microscope must have been the fine abrasive—
grit enlarged. It was years before I saw a recognizable, whole diatom. The kit's diatomaceous earth was a bust.

All that winter I played with the microscope. I prepared slides from things at hand, as the books suggested. I looked at the transparent membrane inside an onion's skin and saw the cells. I looked at a section of cork and saw the cells, and at scrapings from the inside of my cheek, ditto. I looked at my blood and saw not much; I looked at my urine and saw long iridescent crystals, for the drop had dried.

All this was very well, but I wanted to see the wildlife I had read about. I wanted especially to see the famous amoeba, who had eluded me. He was supposed to live in the hay infusion, but I hadn't found him there. He lived outside in warm ponds and streams, too, but I lived in Pittsburgh, and it had been a cold winter.

Finally late that spring I saw an amoeba. The week before, I had gathered puddle water from Frick Park; it had been festering in a jar in the basement. This June night after dinner I figured I had waited long enough. In the basement at my microscope table I spread a scummy drop of Frick Park puddle water on a slide, peeked in, and lo, there was the famous amoeba. He was as blobby and grainy as his picture; I would have known him anywhere.

Before I had watched him at all, I ran upstairs. My parents were still at the table, drinking coffee. They, too, could see the famous amoeba. I told them, bursting, that he was all set up, that they should hurry before his water dried. It was the chance of a lifetime.

Father had stretched out his long legs and was tilting back in his chair. Mother sat with her knees crossed, in blue slacks, smoking a Chesterfield. The dessert dishes were still on the table. My sisters were nowhere in evidence. It was a warm evening; the big dining-room windows gave onto blooming rhododendrons.

Mother regarded me warmly. She gave me to understand that she was glad I had found what I had been looking for, but that she and Father were happy to sit with their coffee, and would not be coming down.

She did not say, but I understood at once, that they had their pursuits (coffee?) and I had mine. She did not say, but I began to understand then, that you do what you do out of your private passion for the thing itself.

I had essentially been handed my own life. In subsequent years my parents would praise my drawings and poems, and supply me with books, art supplies, and sports equipment, and listen to my troubles and enthusiasms, and supervise my hours, and discuss and inform, but they would not get involved with my detective work, nor hear about my reading, nor inquire about my homework or term papers or exams, nor visit the salamanders I caught, nor listen to me play the piano, nor attend my field hockey games, nor fuss over my insect collection with me, or my poetry collection or stamp collection or rock collection. My days and nights were my own to plan and fill.

When I left the dining room that evening and started down the dark basement stairs, I had a life. I sat [next] to my wonderful amoeba, and there he was, rolling his grains more slowly now, extending an arc of his edge for a foot and drawing himself along by that foot, and absorbing it again and rolling on. I gave him some more pond water.

I had hit pay dirt. For all I knew, there were paramecia, too, in that pond water, or daphniae, or stentors, or any of the many other creatures I had read about and never seen: volvox, the spherical algal colony; euglena with its one red eye; the elusive, glassy diatom; hydra, rotifers, water bears, worms. Anything was possible. The sky was the limit.

Response and Analysis

1. How does Annie Dillard respond to her parents' not going to see the amoeba? Why do you think she responded in this way? Dillard writes, "I began to understand then, that you do what you do out of your private passion for the thing itself." What does she mean by this? Why do you think Dillard found delight in using the microscope?

2. How was young Dillard "handed her own life"? Do you remember an incident with your parents, your guardian, or a teacher in which you realized that you had been handed your own life? Briefly describe the incident.

3. Briefly describe young Dillard's level of task commitment, persistence, enthusiasm, and creativity. Are these characteristics positively or negatively related to intelligence? Why or why not?

Research

Suppose you would like to know if children who score low in achievement motivation set different goals for themselves than do children who score high in achievement motivation. After securing approval for your study from the Institutional Review Board at your college or university and from the children's parents, you administer a test measuring achievement motivation to forty eight-year-old children. Next, based on the children's answers, you classify each child as being either low or high in achievement motivation.

You then ask each child, one at a time, to play a miniature bowling game. You tell the child that the object of the game is to knock down as many of the three plastic bowling pins as possible with each roll of a plastic bowling ball. You allow the child to roll the ball ten times and to choose where to stand before rolling the ball. For each roll, you record where the child stands: (a) very close to the pins so that the game is easy, (b) at an intermediate distance so that the game is challenging, or (c) far away so that the game is difficult.

Where do you expect children who score high in achievement motivation and children who score low in achievement motivation to stand? Why? Suppose you knew the child's achievement motivation score. Might knowing the score influence how you record the location at which the child stands? Why or why not? How could you modify the procedure to guarantee that your observations would not be influenced by the child's score?

HELPING CHILDREN AVOID DEPRESSION

Martin E. P. Seligman with Karen Reivich,
Lisa Jaycox, and Jane Gillham

Developmental Concepts
childhood depression, coping skills, applied research

Clinical depression by its very nature is debilitating, and when young children suffer from it, their schoolwork can falter, as can their relations with family and friends. Martin E. P. Seligman, researcher, teacher, and past president of the American Psychological Association, and his colleagues assessed a program designed to help fifth- and sixth-grade students at risk for depression. The investigators first identified those having difficulties. Next, they selected a control group. Their program followed children through high school and provided training sessions for them. These sessions focused on problems the children were having and offered strategies for coping. This selection includes two stories of children who were at risk for depression.

Encouraged by the results of our pilot study with a small group of fifth- and sixth-graders, we were now ready to find a school district to launch the full-scale project. We decided to target Abington, a tree-lined, middle-class suburb outside of Philadelphia, as our first choice. At a lecture I have given to eastern Pennsylvania's leading school superintendents, Dr. Louis Hebert, Abington's superintendent of schools, impressed me enormously with his bold questions and his eagerness to be part of a major change in the education of young teenagers. Abington's location was also convenient for Karen, Lisa, and Jane, the key players. We arranged to meet with Dr. Hebert and Dr. Amy Sichel, the director of pupil services, to discuss the details of the project.

As administrators of an entire school system, Drs. Hebert and Sichel understandably worried about what parents and members of the school board would think of our identifying kids at risk for depression and then offering to help only half of them—leaving the other half to fend for themselves. Finally, we reached a compromise. We agreed to use a "wait-list" control group. We would include seventy children in the coping skills course and thirty children in the wait-list control group. After one year, the children who were assigned to the control group would participate in the same course the seventy children participated in the year before. Instead of being denied the opportunity to participate in the coping skills course, the control children would be given delayed entry into the program after one year. This solution satisfied the Abington officials, but not us.

Our concern was long-term prevention, and if we had a comparison group for only one year, we could not find out if we brought about long-term prevention of depression. The results of school-based programs, and of therapy, usually fade—sometimes they fade fast. It was our mission to develop a program that changes the trajectory of these kids' lives, and we needed a long-term control group that we could follow through high school. Research shows that the rate of depression rises dramatically as children traverse puberty. Without being able to make the critical comparisons across puberty, any prevention claims we might make would be easy to challenge.

We decided to form a long-term control group from another district that closely matched Abington in income, education, and racial composition. This was not a perfect solution, but it was a good second choice. Another nearby school district signed up. We agreed to run the program, improved by its trial run in Abington, for children in this district after the Abington phase of the project was completed. . . .

Children at Risk

The first step in our program was to identify children who were prone to depression. There are a number of factors that increase a child's risk: having a depressed parent, undergoing the death of one's mother, exhibiting low-level depressive symptoms, and living with a family that fights a lot, among others. Since it is hard to find out about parental depression and there were, fortunately, not many maternal deaths in Abington, we focused on the last two factors in order to include as many children as possible.

The actual screening process was quick and simple. Two questionnaires, one that measured symptoms of depression and one that measured the child's perceptions of family conflict, were given to each child whose parents consented. Because our screening method did not require lengthy interviews, we could administer the questionnaires to a group of twenty children in twenty minutes.

The Groups Begin

In the winter of 1990 the Penn Prevention Program officially began. Lisa, Jane, and Karen screened two hundred fifth- and sixth-grade children in the Abington school district and offered spots in the program to seventy children who were at greatest risk for depression. The seventy children were divided into six groups; Lisa, Jane, and Karen each taught two. To ensure that each group was being taught the same material, we developed a minute-by-minute manual that scripted each session. We also videotaped each session so that we could monitor how closely we followed the manuals and evaluate our teaching.

Over dinner before the first day, the research team talked about our work and shared our excitement and nervousness over being in the classroom with the kids at last. We had spent two years developing the program; the following day marked the first time we would actually run the program from start to finish with a group of children at risk for depression. Bringing science to the community is a thrilling endeavor. It is also an awesome responsibility. As we thought about entering the lives of these seventy children, I recalled my conversation with Jonas Salk and hoped that these first-ever trials of psychological immunization would live up to his noble legacy.

We continued to run our groups throughout the winter and spring of that year. Each group had a slightly different personality. One was particularly cohesive and outgoing. This group threw Karen a surprise birthday party, complete with handmade gifts and home-baked cookies. It was a complete surprise, since her birthday wasn't for another four months. Another group was quiet but learned the skills with great precision. A third group could be biting and treated one another roughly. The assertiveness skills were particularly helpful for them. We had hoped that we would become a part of their lives, and we were unprepared for how much they became a part of ours.

Many of the children shared similar family experiences. Since one of our screening criteria was family conflict, many of the children lived with separated or divorced parents who fought a lot. Each child, however, also had his or her own story. The mother of one fifth-grade boy was badly hurt in a car crash and his father, bitter about this ugly turn of fate, was often unavailable to his son. Toby entered our program believing that he had done something to make his father hate him. He constantly ruminated about what it was that he had done, hoping that if he knew his wrongdoing he could make amends.

> It's horrible at my house. My mom is real sick and can't get out of bed. We set up this bed in the living room so that she can see more people and everything but it's still really hard on her. My older sister is thinking of coming home from her college to help out, but my mom doesn't want her to miss out on school. The thing that really bothers me is that my dad won't hardly even talk to me anymore. I know sometimes I get into trouble and that makes Mom and Dad mad, but I can't even figure out what I did this time. Usually I know when I did something wrong, like picked a fight with Mark or got a bad grade in Mr. Bowman's class, but I really don't know this time. I even asked my dad a couple times, but he just says I didn't do anything, but I know I must have. He wouldn't be so mad at me if I didn't do anything.

Toby's home life was in crisis. While our program could not change the dreadful reality of his situation, we could help Toby learn to stop blaming himself for the chaos and strengthen his mental resources for dealing with loss and pain. Toby describes the changes he saw in himself:

Things are still pretty rotten at home. My sister took the semester off from Beaver and that's helping a little. And I guess things are a little better between Dad and me, but not much. But I learned how to stop blaming myself for it all the time. The detective games we played helped me to figure out if I'm blaming myself too much. Sometimes when I start thinking that everything is all my fault, I remember to do the things we did in class and that helps. Like a couple of nights ago I was in my bed and I kept thinking that I must have done something bad, 'cause why else would all this bad stuff be happening to my family. I kept thinking about all the bad things I had ever done and then I really started to feel bad. So anyway, I remembered Karen showing me how to look for evidence like Sherlock and I started to do that. I was gonna turn on my light and try to write it down, but I just did it in my head instead. And it really helped. I could think up lots of good things I do, ways I help Mom out around the house and help Dad cook and things, and that made me feel a lot better. Sometimes I forget to do the Sherlock thing when I'm feeling really bad, but it helps a lot when I remember to do it.

A sixth-grade girl in the program had recently found out that she had been adopted. Miriam felt as though her whole world had changed. Nothing seemed the same and she was furious at her parents for not telling her sooner.

I can remember everything perfectly about the day they told me. I was over at Glenn's house playing with his guinea pigs when my mom called me and told me to come home. Her voice sounded a little weird and I thought she had found out that I had been making crank calls to Danielle Davis. I figured I was going to get grounded or something. Anyway, when I went inside, both my mom and dad were there and they told me to come into the living room and sit down. Now I got really scared, because they both looked so serious, and usually when I get caught doing something wrong, they just start yelling at me right away. They never have me sit down or anything. So anyway, we sit down in the living room and my mom starts off by saying, "Miriam, your father and I love you very much and we want to talk to you about something important."

I was expecting them to say that they were getting a divorce or something. I mean, it's not like they fought a lot, but a couple of my friends' parents got divorced, and the way they were talking—it just sounded like it had to be something like that. When they told me I was adopted, I almost died. I didn't even believe them for the longest time. I just kept sitting there thinking, "Man, they've lost it. I can't believe they're playing such a sick joke on me." Finally, it kind of just sunk in and I knew it must be true and then I was really, really, really mad. I mean, definitely the maddest I have ever been. The only reason they even told me was that Jonathan[1] had been snooping around in my father's office and found some papers in the back of his big black filing cabinet that said something about me being adopted and they were afraid that I might find out and so they wanted me to hear it from them and everything. If it wasn't for Jonathan, I'd still be thinking that I was a real Cooper.

---

[1]Jonathan: Miriam's brother.

During the course of the program, Miriam's primary focus was on the fact that her parents had kept the information from her until recently. She believed that they had conspired together to keep her in the dark and that they would never have told her if her brother hadn't happened to find out. Miriam was so furious at her parents that she refused to talk to them about it and spent as much of her time as she could in her bedroom or at a friend's house.

Throughout the program, we helped Miriam to take a more flexible view of her parents' motivations. This reduced her anger at them and enabled her to talk to them about how she was feeling.

> I really liked coming to the program. Jane was really nice and she helped me a lot. The biggest thing she helped me with was this whole adoption thing. I was so mad at my parents I didn't even want to be in the same room as them. I would come home from school and either go over to Sarah's house or just go into my room and close the door. I guess I was kind of giving them the silent treatment. I know that is pretty childish but I couldn't help it. I mean, I would sit at the dinner table and I would have to keep telling myself over and over and over, "Don't do anything stupid. Just eat your food and keep your mouth shut." I tell you, I really wanted to pick up the food and hurl it at them.
>
> Jane helped me to slow my thinking down so that I could find out what I was saying to myself about the whole thing. I thought that if they really loved me that they would have told me right away, and that since the only reason they did tell was 'cause of Jonathan, that they probably weren't even planning to ever tell me. But Jane helped me think up lots of different reasons why they didn't tell me earlier and reasons why they might have decided to wait until I was even older. You know, like maybe they wanted to make sure I was old enough to understand, or maybe they were scared that I would feel bad if I knew and so they didn't want to tell me. There were, like, seven different reasons I could come up with. After I started thinking about these different things, I didn't feel so mad and I even started asking them some questions about it.

After spending twenty-four hours with these children over twelve weeks, hearing their stories and helping to improve their coping abilities, it was hard to say goodbye. It would have been nice to call the kids every once in a while to say hello and find out how they were doing. But because this was a research project designed to assess whether the twelve-week course could have lasting antidepressive effects for the children, we knew that once the program ended, we could not treat the children who participated in the course any differently than the children who were in the control group.

The Results

For the next two years, we returned to the schools to take measures of the children's symptoms of depression. The program had a clear and immediate effect on depression. Before the program started, 24 percent of the children in both the control group and the prevention group had moderate-to-severe depressive symptoms.

Immediately after the program ended, the prevention group was down to 13 percent, but the control group stayed at 23 percent. Since our program was designed to prevent depression, it was the long-term data that we were most interested in, not the immediate relief the program brought about. If we found that our program reduced depression immediately but did not lead to lasting changes, we would have failed. Our aim was to teach the children a set of skills that they could use throughout their lives. We believed that once the children started using these skills, they would begin to have more mastery and fewer failures, which would improve their mood and reinforce the use of the skills. We wanted to create the upward spiral of a self-reinforcing system.

Every six months we analyzed our data and each time we found that prevention worked. Two years after the program ended, only 22 percent of the children who participated in the coping skills course reported moderate-to-severe depressive symptoms. In contrast, 44 percent of the control group was experiencing this level of symptoms. Two years after saying goodbye to the children, with the only intervening contact being our regular six-month assessments, the children in the prevention groups were half as likely to be depressed.

There are two facts you need to know to put these results in perspective. First, it is nearly a universal finding that the positive effects of all psychological treatments wane over time. This is hardly surprising. People forget what they have learned. They return to environments that aggravate their problems. They no longer get the support and encouragement of their trainers. While we hoped that our program would lead to lasting change, based on the literature, the most reasonable expectation was that our program would peak early and then fade. The second fact is that depression steadily increases as children go through puberty, and the rate of depression is higher in adolescence than it is in childhood. So we expected that the number of children with depressive symptoms would go up across the follow-up period. We hoped that our program would reduce this trend.

Now let's revisit our results. Immediately after the program ended, we had reduced by 35 percent the number of children experiencing strong depressive symptoms. Two years later, we had reduced the number of children with strong depressive symptoms by 100 percent. But the overall trend of depression as the children went through puberty was upward. Over time, however, children in the control group showed a much greater increase in their depressive symptoms than the prevention group. The Penn Prevention Program markedly slowed the natural increase in depression. Our program was the exception to the rule: the prevention effect of our program got bigger over time.

The first question we asked was "Did our program prevent depression?" The answer was yes. The next question we asked was "Did our program increase children's optimism?" Again, the answer was yes. . . . We found consistently that the children in the prevention groups were much less likely to explain bad events pessimistically. In particular, the program helped them undercut their tendency to attribute their problems to permanent causes.

Response and Analysis

1. What family experiences did many of the children report having that may have placed them at risk of depression? According to Martin Seligman and his colleagues, what other factors might increase a child's risk of depression? Why might these factors make a child vulnerable to depression?

2. Briefly describe the coping strategies and other techniques the Seligman team offer to the children at risk of depression. Why do the children participating in the program believe the coping strategies and techniques are effective? Do you think similar techniques would be effective with adults? Why or why not?

3. Why is it important that the researchers follow the students through high school?

What might the researchers learn through long-term involvement and follow-up?

Research

Suppose you want to replicate the study conducted by Seligman and his colleagues at a junior high school and high school in your community. To conduct such a study, you need to secure the permission of the school board, the school administrators, teachers, and parents. You need to provide these persons with an overview of the study. Write a one- to two-paragraph description of the study's purpose and procedures. In writing this overview, keep in mind the following questions: What concerns might parents have? If you were a parent, what concerns might you have? How could researchers address these concerns?

ADOLESCENCE

A few nights in your life, you know this like
the taste of lightning in your teeth:
Tomorrow I will be changed. Somehow in
the next passage of life, I will shed reptilian
skin and feel the wind's friction again.
Sparks will fly. It's a hope for the right
kind of fear, the kind that does not turn
away.

KIM STAFFORD, *Having Everything Right*

Adolescence is a time of transitions and adjustments. Growth spurts and rapid sexual maturation can leave adolescents feeling awkward and unfamiliar with their bodies but also proud of their new capabilities. Cognitive changes allow for more logical, scientific, and abstract thinking, daydreaming, and fantasy.

Adolescents often look to peers for confirmation, intimacy, and support, and they often worry about being liked. Throughout adolescence, parents remain a strong potential source of influence, but the ways in which parents exert influence must be renegotiated often. Teens experience eagerness and anxiety as they prepare to live independent of parents for the first time. Although the teen years have been characterized as a period of "storm and stress," current research suggests that most adolescents maintain favorable self-images and rewarding interpersonal relationships.

Nora Ephron describes her entry into puberty. She becomes convinced that her worries over being feminine will end once her breasts grow. But, compared to her peers, Ephron is slow to develop. She goes through much of her adolescence waiting, comparing herself unfavorably with her peers. There is much variability in the timing of puberty and physical development during adolescence, and many adolescents, like Ephron, are self-conscious about being outside of the averages. Sometimes the effects of early or late maturation on one's identity can last well into adulthood. With the benefit of years, Ephron is able to look back and take a more objective view of her adolescence.

Body image and social relations can be so important that some adolescents go to unhealthy extremes. Determined to be a football star, D. H. starts using steroids to increase his size and strength. Predictably, however, the drug ultimately brings more problems than rewards. It is a paradox that most adolescents develop sophisticated reasoning skills, yet they often fail to recognize or appreciate the consequences of their own risky behaviors. Peer and cultural influences can increase the pressures on adolescents, as D. H. discovers when he enters college and learns that his roommate is a 250-pound linebacker. How do teens cope with the pressures to be high achievers, physically attractive, and popular?

Gretchen Dee reflects on her ambivalence over independence and social relations. Dee has strong family ties and is academically successful, but her concerns about independence, social acceptance, and being attractive contribute to what Dee calls her "bad relationship with food." She perceives herself to be overweight, diets and binges, and feels her self-esteem suffer because of her body image. The extreme concern over appearance can contribute to a pattern of diet-related problems for adolescents and young adults. If unchecked, the problems can lead to psychological disorders such as anorexia nervosa or bulimia nervosa. Dee sometimes treats her concerns philosophically or lightly, and she has developed adult-like aspirations and concerns for the world. She has one foot in adolescence and one foot in early adulthood.

Peer groups are important to Michael Huang, a teenager who immigrated with his family to the United States and who describes himself as half-Chinese and half-Vietnamese. Huang is nearly sixteen, and his keen observations on adolescence and on the cultural differences between his own and his parents' worlds show that he has moved past the earliest stages of adolescence. He understands much about how his parents came to be the people they are and why they attempt to raise him as they do. He reflects on his own thinking (a process called *metacognition*), noting that adolescents like to think that they know everything because they know so much more than they did only a few years before. He sees why, only a year or two earlier, he was much more susceptible to negative peer influences than he is today. Huang's comments show cognition and secure identity formation that often are seen in later stages of adolescence.

Successful physical, cognitive, and emotional development often depend on having the right environmental conditions. Fortunately, most children receive enough support to make successful journeys through adolescence. But what about children who grow up in a "war zone"? That's how LeAlan Jones and Lloyd Newman describe their Chicago neighborhood. Only thirteen and fourteen years old, they have seen gang wars, drug deals, broken families, and broken communities. LeAlan's sister, who is seventeen and has a two-year-old baby, estimates that thirty or forty of her friends have been killed. Poverty has negative effects on development, but environments full of impulsive violence, sex, and drugs are even more likely to produce troubled adolescents. With whom do these children identify? What supports and incentives are available? What adult roles appear as realistic options for these children? Their story, full of surprising candor and insight, underscores the importance of the environment in development.

The final selection is the remarkable tale of two teenage boys, ages fifteen and seventeen, who rebuilt a small plane and flew it across the United States. Rinker Buck describes how he and his older brother Kern formed the idea and presented it to their father, who was initially skeptical. The brothers were very different in temperament and in the way they experienced adolescence. Kern was conscientious and almost painfully shy, while Rinker was outgoing and, at times, openly rebellious, especially toward their strong-willed father. Yet both boys are eager to demonstrate their independence. In the process, they learn much about their relationship with their parents, about each other, and about themselves.

SHAPING UP ABSURD

Nora Ephron

Developmental Concepts
physical development, body image, conformity

Nora Ephron, author of *Sleepless in Seattle* and director of *You've Got Mail*, humorously describes her early adolescence when she was without breasts or hips that could hold up a skirt. Ephron says that she was a late bloomer; embarrassed, she was driven to deceive others into thinking she had physically matured. At all stages of life, many people feel pressure to meet certain standards of attractiveness, but Ephron tells of the special pain for adolescents who believe they fail to meet those standards.

I have to begin with a few words about androgyny. In grammar school, in the fifth and sixth grades, we were all tyrannized by a rigid set of rules that supposedly determined whether we were boys or girls. The episode in *Huckleberry Finn* where Huck is disguised as a girl and gives himself away by the way he threads a needle and catches a ball—that kind of thing. We learned that the way you sat, crossed your legs, held a cigarette and looked at your nails, your wristwatch, the way you did these things instinctively was absolute proof of your sex. Now obviously most children did not take this literally, but I did. I thought that just one slip, just one incorrect cross of my legs or flick of an imaginary cigarette ash would turn me from whatever I was into the other thing; that would be all it took, really. Even though I was outwardly a girl and had many of the trappings generally associated with the field of girldom—a girl's name, for example, and dresses, my own telephone, an autograph book—I spent three early years of my adolescence absolutely certain that I might at any point gum it up. I did not feel at all like a girl. I was boyish. I was athletic, ambitious, outspoken, competitive, noisy, rambunctious. I had scabs on my knees and my socks slid into my loafers and I could throw a football. I wanted desperately not to be that way, not to be a mixture of both things but instead just one, a girl, a definite indisputable girl. As soft and as pink as a nursery. And nothing would do that for me, I felt, but breasts.

I was about six months younger than everyone in my class, and so for about six months after it began, for six months after my friends had begun to develop—that was the word we used, develop—I was not particularly worried. I would sit in the bathtub and look down at my breasts and know that any day now, any second now, they would start growing like everyone else's. They didn't. "I want to buy a bra," I said to my mother one night. "What for?" she said. My mother was really hateful about bras, and by the time my third sister had gotten to that point where she was ready to want one, my mother had worked the whole business into a comedy routine. "Why not use a Band-Aid instead?" she would say. It was a source of great pride to my mother that she had never even had to wear a brassiere until she had her fourth child, and then only because her gynecologist made her. It was incomprehensible to me that anyone would ever be proud of something like that. . . .

I suppose that for most girls, breasts, brassieres, that entire thing, has more trauma, more to do with the coming of adolescence, of becoming a woman, than anything else. Certainly more than getting your period, although that too was traumatic, symbolic. But you could *see* breasts; they were there; they were visible. Whereas a girl could claim to have her period for months before she actually got it and nobody would ever know the difference. Which is exactly what I did. All you had to do was make a great fuss over having enough nickels for the Kotex machine and walk around clutching your stomach and moaning for three to five days a month about The Curse and you could convince anybody. There is a school of thought somewhere in the women's lib/women's mag/gynecology establishment that claims that menstrual cramps are purely psychological, and I lean toward it. Not that I didn't have them finally. Agonizing cramps, heating-pad cramps, go-down-to-the-school-nurse-and-lie-on-the-cot cramps. But unlike any pain I had ever suffered, I adored the pain of cramps, welcomed it, wallowed in it, bragged about it. "I can't go. I have cramps." "I can't do that. I have cramps." And most of all, gigglingly, blushingly: "I can't swim. I have cramps." Nobody ever used the hard-core word. Menstruation. God, what an awful word. Never that. "I have cramps."

The morning I first got my period, I went into my mother's bedroom to tell her. And my mother, my utterly-hateful-about-bras mother, burst into tears. It was really a lovely moment, and I remember it so clearly not just because it was one of the two times I ever saw my mother cry on my account (the other was when I was caught being a six-year-old kleptomaniac), but also because the incident did not mean to me what it meant to her. Her little girl, her firstborn, had finally become a woman. That was what she was crying about. My reaction to the event, however, was that I might well be a woman in some scientific, textbook sense (and could at least stop faking every month and stop wasting all those nickels). But in another sense—in a visible sense—I was as androgynous and as liable to tip over into boyhood as ever.

I started with a 28AA bra. I don't think they made them any smaller in those days, although I gather that now you can buy bras for five year olds that don't have any cups whatsoever in them; trainer bras they are called. My first brassiere came from Robinson's Department Store in Beverly Hills. I went there alone, shaking, positive they would look me over and smile and tell me to come back next year. An actual fitter took me into the dressing room and stood over me while I took off my blouse and tried the first one on. The little puffs stood out on my chest. "Lean over," said the fitter (to this day I am not sure what fitters in bra departments do except to tell you to lean over). I leaned over, with the fleeting hope that my breasts would miraculously fall out of my body and into the puffs. Nothing. . . .

My best friend in school was Diana Raskob. . . . Diana and I had been best friends since we were seven; we were about equally popular in school (which is to say, not particularly), we had about the same success with boys (extremely intermittent), and we looked much the same. Dark. Tall. Gangly.

It is September, just before school begins. I am eleven years old, about to enter the seventh grade, and Diana and I have not seen each other all summer. I have been to camp and she has been somewhere like Banff with her parents. We are meeting, as we often do, on the street midway between our two houses and we will walk back to Diana's and eat junk and talk about what has happened to each of us that summer. I am walking down Walden Drive in my jeans and my father's shirt hanging out and my old red loafers with the socks falling into them and coming toward me is . . . I take a deep breath . . . a young woman. Diana. Her hair is curled and she has a waist and hips and a bust and she is wearing a straight skirt, an article of clothing I have been repeatedly told I will be unable to wear until I have the hips to hold it up. My jaw drops, and suddenly I am crying, crying hysterically, can't catch my breath sobbing. My best friend has betrayed me. She has gone ahead without me and done it. She has shaped up.

Here are some things I did to help:

Bought a Mark Eden Bust Developer.

Slept on my back for four years.

Splashed cold water on them every night because some French actress said in *Life* magazine that that was what *she* did for her perfect bustline.

Ultimately, I resigned myself to a bad toss and began to wear padded bras. I think about them now, think about all those years in high school I went around in them, my three padded bras, every single one of them with different sized breasts. Each time I changed bras I changed sizes: one week nice perky but not too obtrusive breasts, the next medium-sized slightly pointed ones, the next week knockers, true knockers; all the time, whatever size I was, carrying around this rubberized appendage on my chest that occasionally crashed into a wall and was poked inward and had to be poked outward—I think about all that and wonder how anyone kept a straight face through it. My parents, who normally had no restraints about needling me—why did they say nothing as they watched my chest go up and down? My friends, who would periodically inspect my breasts for signs of growth and reassure me—why didn't they at least counsel consistency? . . .

Buster Klepper was the first boy who ever touched them. He was my boyfriend my senior year of high school. . . . Buster was really very sweet—which is, I know, damning with faint praise, but there it is. I was the editor of the front page of the high-school newspaper and he was editor of the back page; we had to work together, side by side, in the print shop, and that was how it started. On the first date, we went to see *April Love* starring Pat Boone. Then we started going together. Buster had a green coupe, a 1950 Ford with an engine he had handchromed until it shone, dazzled, reflected the image of anyone who looked into it, anyone usually being Buster polishing it or the gas-station attendants he constantly asked to check the oil in order for them to be overwhelmed by the sparkle on the valves. . . .

There was necking. Terrific necking. First in the car, overlooking Los Angeles from what is now the Trousdale Estates. Then on the bed of his parents' cabana at Ocean House. Incredibly wonderful, frustrating necking, I loved it, really, but no further than necking, please don't, please, because there I was absolutely terrified of . . . his finding out there was next to nothing there (which he knew, of course; he wasn't that dumb).

I broke up with him at one point. I think we were apart for about two weeks. At the end of that time I drove down to see a friend at a boarding school in Palos Verdes Estates and a disc jockey played *April Love* on the radio four times during the trip. I took it as a sign. I drove straight back to Griffith Park to a golf tournament Buster was playing in (he was the sixth-seeded teenage golf player in Southern California) and presented myself back to him on the green of the 18th hole. It was all very dramatic. That night we went to a drive-in and I let him get his hand under my protuberances and onto my breasts. He really didn't seem to mind at all. . . .

And even now, now that I have been countlessly reassured that my figure is a good one, now that I am grown up enough to understand that most of my feelings have very little to do with the reality of my shape, I am nonetheless obsessed by breasts. . . .

After I went into therapy, a process that made it possible for me to tell total strangers at cocktail parties that breasts were the hang-up of my life, I was often told that I was insane to have been bothered by my condition. I was also frequently told, by close friends, that I was extremely boring on the subject. And my girlfriends, the ones with nice big breasts, would go on endlessly about how their lives had been far more miserable than mine. Their bra straps were snapped in class. They couldn't sleep on their stomachs. They were stared at whenever the word "mountain" cropped up in geography. And *Evangeline*, good God what they went through every time someone had to stand up and recite the Prologue to Longfellow's *Evangeline*: " . . . *stand like druids of eld . . . With beards that rest on their bosoms.*" It was much worse for them, they tell me. They had a terrible time of it, they assure me. I don't know how lucky I was, they say.

Response and Analysis

1. What was Nora Ephron's conception of gender when she was an adolescent? Do many girls and boys have similar thoughts and beliefs about gender? Why or why not?

2. Why are adolescents so concerned over the appearance of secondary sex characteristics during puberty? What societal influences promote such concerns? What are the most common short-term and long-term psycho-

logical effects of late physical development for girls? For boys? What are the most common effects of early physical development for girls? For boys?

3. What is the relationship between body image and self-esteem in adolescence? Is this relationship different for girls and boys? If so, how? Is the relationship between body image and self-esteem different for various ethnic or cultural groups? If so, in what ways? What might account for these differences?

4. During the past one hundred years, the average age at which children reach puberty has decreased. This downward shift is called the secular trend. Why do you think the secular trend has occurred? What social consequences might it have had? What social consequences might it have if it continues?

Research

Suppose you suspect that improved health care and diet may lead to children growing faster, taller, and stronger, and thus reaching sexual maturity more quickly. How could you test this hypothesis by comparing children in more-developed nations with children in less-developed nations? What characteristics would be important in selecting comparison groups? What factors would you need to control? Could you conduct your study using different regions of the United States? Why or why not?

DYING TO BE BIGGER

D. H.

Developmental Concepts
physical development, body image, achievement motivation, substance abuse, peer pressure

What motivates a person to achieve a goal even at the risk of endangering his or her health? At age fifteen, D. H. is so determined to be a football star that he uses steroids to increase his size and prowess. Ignoring the prescribed dosage, he swallows five pills a day. Within weeks, D. H. notices unpleasant physical and emotional changes; he eventually becomes overly aggressive and, as his condition worsens, almost sterile. With the help of his parents, D. H. quits using steroids for a year. What happens when he enters college and has as his roommate a six-foot-three, 250-pound linebacker? What adjustment problems does D. H. experience after he quits taking steroids?

I was only fifteen years old when I first started maiming my body with the abuse of anabolic steroids. I was always trying to fit in with the "cool" crowd in junior high and high school. Willingly smoking or buying pot when offered, socially drinking in excess, displaying a macho image—and, of course, the infamous "kiss and tell" were essentials in completing my insecure mentality.

Being an immature, cocky kid from a somewhat wealthy family, I wasn't very well liked in general. In light of this, I got beat up a lot, especially in my first year of public high school.

I was one of only three sophomores to get a varsity letter in football. At five-foot-nine and 174 pounds, I was muscularly inferior to the guys on the same athletic level and quite conscious of the fact. So when I heard about this wonderful drug called steroids from a teammate, I didn't think twice about asking to buy some. I could hardly wait to take them and start getting bigger.

I bought three months' worth of Dianobol (an oral form of steroids and one of the most harmful). I paid fifty-five dollars. I was told to take maybe two or three per day. I totally ignored the directions and warnings and immediately started taking five per day. This is how eager I was to be bigger and possibly "cooler."

Within only a week, everything about me started to change. I was transforming mentally and physically. My attention span became almost nonexistent. Along with becoming extremely aggressive, I began to abandon nearly all academic and family responsibilities. In almost no time, I became flustered and agitated with simple everyday activities. My narcissistic ways brought me to engage in verbal as well as physical fights with family, friends, teachers, but mostly strangers.

My bodily transformations were clearly visible. In less than a month, I took the entire three-month supply. I gained nearly thirty pounds. Most of my weight was from water retention, although at the time I believed it to be muscle. Instead of having pimples like the average teenager, my acne took the form of grotesque, cystlike blood clots that would occasionally burst while I was lifting weights. My nipples became the size of grapes and hurt severely, which is common among male steroid users. My hormonal level was completely out of whack.

At first I had such an overload of testosterone that I would have to masturbate daily, at minimum, in order to prevent having "wet dreams." Obviously these factors enhanced my lust, which eventually led to acute perversion. My then almost-horrifying physique prevented me from having any sexual encounters.

All of these factors led to my classification as a wretched menace. My parents grew sick and tired of all the trouble I began to get in. They were scared of me, it seemed. They cared so much about my welfare, education, and state of mind that they sent me to a boarding school that summer.

I could not obtain any more steroids there, and for a couple of months it seemed I had subtle withdrawal symptoms and severe side effects. Most of the time that summer I was either depressed or filled with intense anger, both of which were uncontrollable unless I was in a state of intoxication from any mind-altering drug.

After a year of being steroid-free, things started to look promising for me, and I eventually gained control over myself. Just when I started getting letters from big-name colleges to play football for them, I suffered a herniated disc. I was unable to participate in any form of physical activity the entire school year.

In the fall, I attended a university in the Northeast, where I was on the football team but did not play due to my injury. I lifted weights with the team every day. I wasn't very big at the time, even after many weeks of working out. Once again I found myself to be physically inferior and insecure about my physique. And again came into contact with many teammates using steroids.

My roommate was a six-foot-three, 250-pound linebacker who played on the varsity squad as a freshman. As the weeks passed, I learned of my roommate's heavy steroid use. I was exposed to dozens of different steroids I had never even heard of. Living in the same room with him, I watched his almost daily injections. After months of enduring his drug offerings, I gave in.

By the spring of my freshman year, I had become drastically far from normal in every way. My body had stopped producing hormones due to the amount of synthetic testosterone I injected into my system. At five-foot-eleven, 225 pounds, disproportionately huge, acne-infested, outrageously aggressive, and nearing complete sterility, I was in a terrible state of body and mind. Normal thoughts of my future (not pertaining to football), friends, family, reputation, moral status, etc., were entirely beyond me. My whole entire essence had become one of a primitive barbarian. This was when I was taking something called Sustunon (prepackaged in a syringe labeled "For equine use only") containing four types of testosterone. I was "stacking" (a term used by steroid users which means mixing different types) to get well-cut definition along with mass.

It was around this time when I was arrested for threatening a security guard. When the campus police came to arrest me, they saw how aggressive and large my roommate and I were. So they searched our room and found dozens of bottles and hundreds of dollars' worth of steroids and syringes. We had a trial, and the outcome was that I could only return the next year if I got drug-tested on a monthly basis. I certainly had no will power or desire to quit my steroid abuse, so I transferred schools.

After a summer of even more heavy-duty abuse, I decided to attend a school that would cater to my instinctively backward ways. That fall I entered a large university in the South. Once again I simply lifted weights without being involved in competition or football. It was there that I finally realized how out of hand I'd become with my steroid problem.

Gradually I started to taper down my dosages. Accompanying my reduction, I began to drink more and more. My grades plummeted again. I began going to bars and keg parties on a nightly basis.

My celibacy, mental state, aggressiveness, lack of athletic competition, and alcohol problem brought me to enjoy passing my pain onto others by means of physical aggression. I got into a fight almost every time I drank. In the midst of my insane state, I was arrested for assault. I was in really deep this time. Finally I realized how different from everybody else I'd become, and I decided not to taper off but to quit completely.

The average person seems to think that steroids just make you bigger. But they are a drug, and an addictive one at that. This drug does not put you in a stupor or in a hallucinogenic state but rather gives you an up, all-around "bad-ass" mentality that far exceeds that of either normal life or any other narcotic I've tried when not taking steroids. Only lately are scientists and researchers discovering how addictive steroids are—only now, after hundreds of thousands may have done such extreme damage to their lives, bodies, and minds.

One of the main components of steroid addiction is how unsatisfied the user is with his overall appearance. Although I was massive and had dramatic muscular definition, I was never content with my body, despite frequent compliments. I was always changing types of steroids, places of injection, workouts, diet, etc. I always found myself saying, "This one oughta do it" or "I'll quit when I hit 230 pounds."

When someone is using steroids, he has psychological disorders that increase when usage stops. One disorder is anxiety from the loss of the superior feeling you get from the drug. Losing the muscle mass, high energy level, and superhuman sensation that you're so accustomed to is terrifying.

Another ramification of taking artificial testosterone over time is the effect on the natural testosterone level (thus the male sex drive). As a result of my steroid use, my natural testosterone level was ultimately depleted to the point where my sex drive was drastically reduced in comparison to the average twenty-one-year-old male. My testicles shriveled up, causing physical pain as well as extreme mental anguish. Thus I desired girls less. This however did lead me to treat them as people, not as objects of my desires. It was a beginning step on the way to a more sane and civil mentality.

The worst symptoms of my withdrawal after many months of drug abuse were emotional. My emotions fluctuated dramatically, and I rapidly became more sensitive. My hope is that this feeling of being trailed by isolation and aloneness will diminish and leave me free of its constant haunting.

Response and Analysis

1. Why did D. H. begin and then continue using anabolic steroids even when he knew that they were harmful to him? To what extent was he responding to external pressures on males to be dominant and successful? To what extent was he responding to his own internal achievement motivation?

2. How did D. H.'s body image relate to his sense of self-esteem? In what ways is the relationship between body image and self-esteem likely to be the same for boys as for

girls? In what ways is it likely to be different? Do few, many, or most adolescents develop idealized body images that they cannot attain? Why or why not? Does the failure to attain those images result in psychological or social problems for them? If so, how and why?

3.   Adolescents sometimes experiment with and abuse alcohol and other drugs. What factors most affect whether an adolescent will use or resist using alcohol and drugs?

Research

Suppose you want to know if people who use steroids to enhance their athletic performance have higher achievement motivation than those who do not use steroids. You must decide whether to develop a questionnaire to assess achievement or use existing questionnaires, the reliability and validity of which are known. List three advantages and three disadvantages of (a) using existing questionnaires, and (b) developing your own questionnaire.

ONE FOOT OUT THE DOOR: FACING THE CHALLENGES OF LATE ADOLESCENCE

Sydney Lewis: An interview with Gretchen Dee

Developmental Concepts
    independence, dieting, self-image, importance of
    family and relationships

Gretchen Dee, who was raised in Chicago, describes herself to interviewer Sydney Lewis as having been one of the kids who didn't get into trouble in high school. Dee, now nineteen and a freshman in college, discusses the problems she did have through her teens and those that still plague her. Although she has a good sense of self, she occasionally has doubts about her attractiveness and especially about her weight. In an effort to be trim, she sometimes fasts for a day, but then she weakens and binges the following day. Dee argues that media stereotypes of teenagers and societal pressures to be thin are more detrimental than many people realize. A good student, Dee is interested in political and social issues and raises important questions about her future. To what extent have you had conflicts over appearance, group pressure, and career goals?

I was very successful in my high school. I was always very—not a kissass—but I was interested in my teachers and I cared about the school. I love being protected, but I think there is a natural instinct to move on. That's a really huge part of all these problems that teenagers have with their parents. Like my brother, who's seventeen. My mom says, and I agree, that if we were cavemen he would have his own cave now. My sister just suffers from being the youngest. She's the big rebel, she's the black lipstick and Doc Martens—the punk of the family. She wants to cut and dye her hair. My mom says, "Don't you want long, pretty, curly hair?" [feigns anger] *"I don't want to look like Gretchen, and I don't want a flowered room like Gretchen."* [laughs] So, independence!

But for me, going to college—I didn't want to go. I thought my life was good. I thought, "I have this great trusting relationship with my parents, they're very loose—I have no curfew." I was satisfied with my social life. I was feeling maybe I needed a new start, to get away from all the stereotypes in high school, but it wasn't enough of an urge to overpower the comfortableness with my family and my home.

In high school I was plagued by not having a boyfriend—I really didn't have any serious boyfriends until I got to college. I always had trouble in relationships because I was so outspoken. I had a prom my senior year, and I could've gotten a date, but I was too proud to go with someone that I didn't want to go with. And that will stay with me the rest of my life. I had enough attention, it's that no one ever seemed to want to date me seriously. I felt and still feel every day like I'm not good enough. When I meet a guy I'll be like, "Oh, he'll never like me 'cause I'm not pretty enough or I'm not smart enough." I'm not worthy. I can say to myself, "Look at your grades, look at where you've come in your life," but it doesn't matter—it's still that rejection.

All my friends had boyfriends, always. I don't look at other girls who don't have boyfriends and say, "There's something wrong with that person." But I always felt people looked at me that way. Not just boys, but everyone. "Gretchen has no boyfriend, it must be because there's something wrong with her." I don't know where it comes from, but I have to believe it's partly the fact that you turn on TV or open a magazine and every girl has a boyfriend, every girl is a hundred and twenty pounds, and beautiful. You should be thin, you should have a boyfriend, and you should be smart too. The culture tells you also, not too smart, not too self-empowered, not too independent. And you shouldn't be too good either, because that's not fun.

I've always been at the top of my class academically and involved in volunteer activities. I was Miss Involved, the perfect college candidate. But at the same time, I was so hugely affected by wanting to fit in. I didn't realize how low my self-esteem was, my self-image. I still have body-image problems, I have eating disorders. I'm a self-empowered woman and a feminist, and I believe I can do all these things, and I see how successful I've been in my life—but at the same time I am so affected by not feeling pretty enough, not feeling thin enough.

I've definitely changed a lot going to college. I go to a small college in Minnesota, it's known for being highly liberal and highly intense. As a general rule they get students that were social outcasts in high school—the majority of them are out to be different, weird. It puts me in the absolute norm, and all of a sudden I come off as being really good-looking. What I realized in college was how damaged I was, like emotionally, by the silliest things . . . Like the fact that I didn't make cheerleading when I was younger, or the fact that I always felt fat, and how that had a huge, huge, huge, huge impact on my life. I don't think there's ever been a time, in the last eight years, when I haven't been on a diet. My perspective is: I am heavier than everybody else. [sighs] I'm not anorexic or bulimic, but I definitely have a bad relationship with food.

I never enjoy food, there's always the guilt. Guilt, guilt, guilt. If I eat too much today, then I won't eat tomorrow at all. I weigh myself every single day without fail, and if I gain a pound it affects my mood the whole day. I tie food to emotions. When I'm upset I have two reactions: binge or starve—eat celery and water for a week, or eat a whole pizza. I just can't seem to ever eat normally. When I'm in public—when I go out for dinner, when I am at the college cafeteria—I eat nothing.

My roommates were the ones that said, "Gretchen, something's wrong—you're totally binging." They made me get help, they begged me for months. They were like, "We're calling your parents if you don't." Finally my roommate made the appointment. I said, "Fine, I'll go once"—and I went three times. But oh my God, to this day I'm still denying the fact that I have an eating disorder. Or I see it as, "Lots of people have eating disorders, mine isn't serious—there are people with much worse problems." So when I talk about this it's not me speaking, it's not my true feeling. It's what I've come to accept, and I'm trying to talk myself into it.

How am I gonna stop the "I'm not worthy" stuff? [sighs] You know what is really pathetic? When my therapist asked me that, I answered, "Lose fifteen pounds." [laughs] And part of me believes that if I just lose the weight I'll be OK. Isn't that awful? And I know that's wrong—I know life's not easier for beautiful people. But you get cut a break here and there when you're beautiful: you get more attention, you get taken more seriously. It's no joke that as an overweight person it's harder for you, and that success is sometimes tied to physical appearance.

The media says everyone should be thin and pretty, and I think that's a *huge* influence on all teenagers. There's such a high expectation to be something they can't be. I think they're uncomfortable, they feel kind of dumped on, like the expectations of them are too much. It's the loss of innocence. We have teenagers growing up with adult issues, and they're without all the emotional resources to deal with that. You're still a child in so many ways: you don't have the stability, the self-confidence yet, but you're *forced* to deal with things. There's nothing sacred about being a teenager anymore—you grow up so fast. . . .

I love my parents, we're very close. And they've both worked hard, they're not rich, they're middle-class people. [sighs] Gosh, this is such a big source of guilt with me. [distressed] How am I gonna tell my parents, who paid for my college education and worked hard, that they gotta sacrifice for me? I work every summer, I work over Christmas break, I do everything I can to help pay for my college education. And I hope somehow I'll be economically stable enough to help them out when they're older. That's the way it should work—like it used to in the olden days when kids took care of their parents. . . .

I want to make a lot of money, I want a beautiful house, and children, and a castle, and I want to be able to travel and see the world and be able to send my children to excellent schools. I want that, and I think part of me actually believes I'm gonna have that, but reality-speaking-wise, I know too much. I'll probably have to live in debt, and just make ends meet—especially if I want to work in the political field. I'm gonna drive a secondhand car and live in a small apartment, and probably not go out to dinner, and coupon-clip for the rest of my life. A couple years ago I thought, "I can't settle for that." Now I'm kind of like, "There's nothing wrong with that." I've come to realize that having a job you like is probably the most important thing.

I'm going to Washington, D.C., next term, through a program at school. I'm going to be working on the national deficit with an interest group that's Generation X, twenty-something politics. We're doing Social Security, reform, the environment, infrastructure, education. I was thinking about what I could do when I come back—like maybe talk to high school classes. Going back and just explaining in simple terms, the debt, the deficit, what it means, how it affects you. I know I was scared off by economic terms in high school, but it's not that hard to understand. I want people to know, that is my whole goal. Because they don't really know. And who's to blame? You don't see it on the news, you don't see it in the kids' papers or magazines. What about *Seventeen* magazine? For all their hair and looks and makeup and fashion, what about something on the deficit? The right things are not in the media. There's such an audience: they watch so much TV, they read so many magazines; it'd be so easy to reach them, yet no one's doing it. That's kind of where my focus is going to be.

I'm thinking if I were to have a claim to fame, that's where I'd like to make my name: to start an organization or to spread education—*do something*. Use the power of one human being in a thousand to take the energy and money and time. It amazes me, the power of human beings, one in a thousand, to really do something, to be unselfish. And that's why we're going to be OK—probably.

Response and Analysis

1. Why is Gretchen Dee ambivalent about becoming independent from her parents? Is the kind of ambivalence she describes typical of that of most adolescents who contemplate going to college? Why or why not? What thoughts and feelings were (or are) associated with moving toward independent living for you?

2. What diet-related thoughts and behaviors does Dee have that are healthy? Unhealthy? How do concerns over diet relate to her self-image? Why do adolescent girls and young women in the United States develop problems around diet, self-image, and social relations? Do you think these problems are as prevalent in other countries? Why or why not?

3. Although Dee says she has concerns about her independence, self-image, and social relations, there are many indications that she is a normal, healthy teenager. What characteristics does she present that suggest good mental and physical health? The likelihood that she will adjust well to adult life?

Research

Suppose you conduct a study to investigate the relationship between self-esteem and eating disorders (specifically, anorexia nervosa). After securing the necessary approval, you ask fifty female and fifty male students at a local high school to complete an eating disorders questionnaire and a self-esteem questionnaire. You find that there is a moderate negative correlation ($r = -.22$) between anorexia nervosa and self-esteem. What are three possible explanations for this relationship? Why is it not possible to determine, given the data you have collected, which explanation is correct?

MICHAEL HUANG:
FROM VIETNAM TO AMERICA

Sydney Lewis: An interview with Michael Huang

Developmental Concepts
differentiation, individuation, relationships with
parents, multicultural identity

When Michael Huang was five years old, he and his family immigrated to Chicago from Vietnam. Now at age fifteen, during an interview with writer Sydney Lewis, Huang speaks of the tension between his American lifestyle and the values of his Asian culture. These two very different worlds sometimes puzzle him, the former stressing more allegiance to oneself, the latter allegiance to family and community. Huang's values reflect his upbringing. Unsure of a career, he nonetheless wants to be successful. For him, going to school is a job that will help him reach his goal, and he is willing to delay gratification and work hard to have a better life.

In Vietnamese culture being a teen really has no meaning, because you have like maybe an ounce more freedom than when you were two. The culture is very family oriented. You reach eighteen and start working—you still live with your parents. And then you start raising them, you know what I mean? They raise you, you raise them, and then your children raise you. You are not really an individual, so rebelling and being a teen has no meaning—there's no point in it. Actually, if you do rebel you're looked down upon, and every other teen thinks you're crazy.

I am half-Chinese, half-Vietnamese—both my parents are half-Vietnamese, half-Chinese. I have one sister, she's sixteen, but I have like two billion cousins and uncles and aunts—there's too many of them, actually. [laughs] I grew up in Vietnam, in a suburb of Saigon or Ho Chi Minh City, whatever you want to call it. I don't remember how to read or write Vietnamese—I can speak it though. I guess my life in Vietnam was better than most, because on my mom's side we owned a little motel and pool hall, and a restaurant. On my dad's side we owned an herbal shop that's been in the family for a couple hundred years or something. I'm just waiting for my share of it. [laughs]. . . .

Vietnamese culture is pretty strict: you go to school—that's your job—you go home; you do chores; you do homework; you go to bed. That's not how things work around here, and it's very hard for my parents to accept that. I know exactly where they're coming from, though; the problem is, they don't know what *I'm* talking about. My parents are Americanized, they're not that strict . . . but all these influences around them—my grandma, and her old kind of friends, and old aunts and stuff—mock on my parents: "Why are you letting your kid do this?" My mom, she knows that I'm smart enough to not get in trouble, and she trusts me, but she does not want to disappoint *her* mother.

In Asian culture disappointing your elders is a big taboo. If I do something bad, it's like my whole family has been cursed. I do something bad, my grandma thinks when she walks out in the street people are going to look at her. You are not an individual: your actions affect everyone else. Which is not like the American way: I am myself, so you can kiss my ass for all I care! [laughs] And sometimes I bring that attitude home to my parents, which is terribly wrong. You know, going outside and coming back home are two different worlds—*totally* different. When I'm at school, the American way, I'll talk back to anyone I feel like. Of course, I know better. When I am at home I do not talk back to my parents. But sometimes I forget that I'm at home, [laughs] and I *will* talk back to my mother. I start doing reasoning crap.

I go out a lot, you know, dating. *Big* taboo! Oh, they think dating is the most horrible thing you can do—after sex, which is the *worst* thing you can do in your whole life. I was dating people, and my parents found out . . . after, like, my fifteenth date. Of course, someone snitched on me, or maybe they had a spy following me around—they have like a network thing. And I had to explain to them, it's not like I'm going to marry this person, it's just I'm trying to build a friendship.

They're very heavy on marriages: they want marriages to work, and they don't believe in divorce. And my reasoning is, if you don't want that to happen, I think you've got to train for marriages, and by doing this thing, dating, you train. You learn how to interact with people, how to interact in a relationship; you know what to do and you know how to fight, how to resolve conflict. But they don't believe in reasoning. They're up there, I'm down here: people up there are right, people down here are wrong—that's it, that's all there is to it.

I try to reason with them, and sometimes they listen, but sometimes they act like there's someone over their shoulder saying, "Don't let him talk to you like that. You're the parents, you're in control here! Why are you so scared of your kid?" Culture dictates that a fifteen-year-old does not have a mind of his own, does not have his own ideas. I think it's a matter of control about the Vietnamese culture—I think the elders [claps hands officiously] want control, and once they're losing control they get frustrated. Like when a parent tells a kid to do something and a kid refuses, they feel they're losing control: they get frustrated, they start hitting. Not that hitting is bad, but they start hitting because they don't know what else to do. And if hitting doesn't work, then they just totally give up and they go in their room, and they close the door, and they cry. I guess all parents, not only the Vietnamese, are very good at guilt trips, especially mothers. Guilt trips are a universal method to discipline a kid.

As a teenager, you're in an in-between stage. Your parents are like, "You're grown up," but then, "You're still a kid." You get two contrasting things going. I like to think I know everything, but I really don't. Teenagers think they know everything, because they know much more than they did when they were like nine or ten years old, and that's a really big leap. Since it's such a big leap you think, "Oh, I've reached the pinnacle of knowledge, I can't be any smarter."

Some kids just rebel, because their parents are really strict and don't know how their life is. And there's no way, I mean *no way*, your parents will know what you're going through. You gotta really make the effort to let it be known what's going on with you. But some of these kids, they're frustrated and they don't know what to do. They go home and it's all strict; then they go outside and see how everyone else has freedom, how everyone else has the right to express themselves, and they don't—so they rebel. And that's where the gang thing comes in.

If you walk the other way down Broadway, you'll see by the video rental store so many of them standing there—in the summer outside, and in the winter inside—cause there's an arcade in there. After school, they'll spend like maybe from three to eight there. They don't know where they're going, no direction or anything. They're frustrated, and they feel a sense of hopelessness because they think they're not gonna make it through their teenage years. All those kids, they wear their low, big, baggy clothes and stuff, just to be like everyone else. A lot of parents object to that, but what can they do? My parents would *beat* me if I wore big clothes. [laughs] Not that I want to.

There was a period where I wanted to wear the big pants, and do what everyone else did, but I grew out of that. I was thirteen or fourteen. I saw these things when I was going to school, and I thought, "They're doing it, so why can't I?" Big pants, smoking, sex, and all that stuff. You know, "Everyone's doing it—so many people can't be wrong." People who follow the crowd are still developing their sense of self-worth. I guess I've developed a sense that I'm worth this much, and I will not lower my price by doing what everyone else does—because then I'll be just a duplicate, and not an original.

I was a pretty good child, pretty well disciplined. Third, fourth, fifth, and sixth grade I was around the neighborhood, but seventh and eighth grade I went to a private, rich, kind of snobby-people school. We weren't rich, and you see all these kids who were spending money like it was water, and were kind of ignorant about things, kind of insensitive, not aware that there are homeless people on earth. . . .

I felt kind of out of place. When I first went there I wasn't with the in-crowd, but I started hanging out with them. [softly] Sometimes I felt like a lesser person—because they're rich, they're smart, and they're beautiful people—physically beautiful. They're kind of like a clique, in-crowd thing. When you get to hang out with the in-crowd you get this sense of superiority over the rest, and I started getting into these snobby ways. I hung out with Doug a lot for some reason. I guess it kind of made me feel like I was climbing the social ladder. You know, "Oh, I'm hanging out at his high-rise condo over the Lake and swimming in his swimming pool." But then you feel like a phony.

I didn't invite any of those kids to my house. I was kind of embarrassed then, 'cause you go to these people's houses and they have antiques and handmade rugs and stuff. And they come to your house, you have an average kind of house, with average kind of things. And they probably don't notice, but you have that illusion. You do this "what if?" thing. "What if they come to my house and they see these things? Would they think less of me?" That school clouded my mind. I was kind of lost there for a while.

There was a period, thirteen, fourteen, when I did pickpocketing, and theft and stuff, shoplifting. . . . The first thing I ever stole was baseball cards—which was really stupid—and then I started stealing bigger stuff, like packs of pens and pencils, binders, school-related things—for my education, of course! [laughs] I got caught stealing clothes once. I was taken to the station. My parents don't know. I'll tell them eventually, when I become a very successful person who turns out to be very moral and ethical. I'll say, "I did all these bad things, and in spite of all the bad things I did, I turned out good." I think you learn from your mistakes.

I guess friends do influence you a lot—I was hanging around with the rich white snobby kids; they were doing it for the thrill. I wasn't missing anything at home, and it's not like my parents didn't buy me clothes. I guess I just did it to rebel, and to belong; "Yeah, stealing is *good*." [laughs] I knew it was wrong. It was kind of like a "so what, oh well" attitude that I had. A lot of people have this "so what" attitude. . . .

A definition of success to me—one of the most important things—is happiness. You can be living in a cardboard box, and if you're happy with it, you are successful. But I think success is enhanced with money. Money is just icing on the cake. I am materialistic—I admit that—but I care about community issues and stuff. If I can't help society, I'm not gonna make the problem worse by being bad myself.

I have a plan, I have a goal. I have several goals actually . . . [laughs] But I'm not sure about anything yet. Before, I thought of being something in the medical field—a pediatrician, a brain surgeon. [laughs] But I'm more of a brain donor. Well, now I'm looking at a more realistic goal, because I know I'm not going to be able to stay in school for, like, another ten years after college—I'm not a school person. I'm thinking of maybe journalism, broadcasting, radio, or maybe writing a book. But I know what I want to do, and that is to become successful—and *that* is to become happy.

Response and Analysis

1. Michael Huang describes differences between his parents' native culture and practices prevalent in the United States. What differences does he observe in terms of family structure, parenting practices, and obligation to obey and please one's elders? How might these differences influence psychosocial development during adolescence?

2. Why does Huang believe that teenagers think they know everything? How does he describe himself in this regard? Based on Huang's discussion of teen thinking, what are your impressions of the level of Huang's egocentrism? At what stage in the development

of adolescent thinking does he seem to be? What evidence supports your view?

3. Huang suggests that parents often don't know how life is for teenagers. Do you agree? Why or why not? Why might it be difficult for parents to know what life is like for teens today?

4. Huang says that there was a period during which he practiced thievery, including pick-pocketing and shoplifting. What motivated him to commit petty crimes? What types of law-breaking behaviors are most common during adolescence? What factors influence whether an adolescent will continue or abandon criminal behavior?

Research

Cross-cultural studies of adolescent development help establish which aspects of development are universal and which are culturally bound. Suppose you want to conduct a cross-cultural study by interviewing high-school exchange students in your community. You need to identify students to interview, secure all necessary permissions, and decide how to interview the students. You decide to use a standard interview protocol and ask the same questions of all the interviewees. Write five questions that you would ask the participants. Why is it important to make the participants feel comfortable and willing to talk? In what type of environment would you interview the participants? Why? How would you record their responses? Why? How do you think your own ethnicity, gender, and style of dress might influence the participants' responses and their willingness to disclose information about themselves?

OUR AMERICA: LIFE AND DEATH ON THE SOUTH SIDE OF CHICAGO

LeAlan Jones and Lloyd Newman

Developmental Concepts
coping with poverty, gangs, substance abuse, violence;
moral development; courage

LeAlan Jones and Lloyd Newman were thirteen and fourteen years old when producer David Isay invited them to participate in a Public Broadcast System documentary series, *Chicago Matters*. For seven days in March 1993, the boys interviewed family and friends and gave running commentary about their neighborhood and school in the ghetto. Jones and Newman, who have been close friends for several years, reveal despair and fortitude, humor and wisdom in their observations. Life in their neighborhood is a "war zone," and these children hope they will survive to adulthood, but they have no unrealistic expectations. Here, Jones introduces his family and his world. He doesn't know his father and says he has no need of him now, stating that he has lived half his life without him. Jones's mother suffers from bipolar disorder, and he worries about his older sister who at age seventeen has a two-year-old baby. Jones's strong support is his grandmother, who has lived in their home since 1937.

Our neighborhood is a fun neighborhood if you know what you're doing. If you act like a little kid in this neighborhood, you're not gonna last too long. 'Cause if you play childish games in the ghetto, you're gonna find a childish bullet in your childish brain. If you live in the ghetto, when you're ten you know everything you're not supposed to know. When I was ten I knew where drugs came from. I knew about every different kind of gun. I knew about sex. I was a kid in age but my mind had the reality of a grown-up, 'cause I seen these things every day!

Like when I was eight years old, my cousin Willy had a friend named Baby Tony and another friend, Little Cecil. They used to hang out—watch TV, go to the park and hoop, sell drugs. They all went to jail. When Baby Tony came out he was walking through the park when a boy lit him up and blew his face off. His face was *entirely* blown off. And then a couple of days later Little Cecil sold somebody a dummy bag of plaster from off the walls, so the man who was using it came back and asked him for his money back. Little Cecil took off running and the man shot him. And Cecil was dead. That was both of my cousin's friends that died in one week! And I heard about this when I was *eight!* I had just seen Baby Tony the day before he died.

It's like Vietnam. I remember one time I was over at my auntie's house spending the night. We were playing Super Nintendo and I heard this lady say, "I heard you been looking for me, nigger!" Then she just—BOOM! BOOM! BOOM! BOOM! She let off about eight shots. Then I heard the other gun fire off. And we were just still there playing like nothing happened. In Vietnam, them people came back crazy. I live in Vietnam, so what you think I'm gonna be if I live in it and they just went and visited? Living around here is depressing! It's depressing! Just look outside—this isn't Wally and the Beaver!

*   *   *   *   *

It's Friday afternoon after school, and we're going to take you on a tour of our neighborhood. It's about sixty degrees today—feels good out. Walking down the streets. See an abandoned building, graffiti on the wall. See some little kids playing on a little shopping cart that they got from Jewel Supermarket.

Walking by some abandoned houses—looks like some Scud missiles just bombed them out. A lot of trash here—glass and things. Used to be little snakes in this field in the summertime and we'd catch them. People out here pitching pennies. Houses boarded up.

Walking through puddles of water. Bums on the street. An abandoned church. A helicopter. There goes somebody we thought was dead—guess he ain't dead.

By the old library, which is no longer in business—there was a murder in there last year and they closed it down. See a "Rest in Peace" sign. Birds flying. There's the store that they burned down when the Bulls won the championship. Going by the gas station where they sell liquor and food. Now we see some spray paint that says: "Justice for Rodney King/Revolution Is the Only Solution."

Now we're walking in the Ida Bees,[1] which is 50 percent boarded up. Now we're by Lloyd's house. Abandoned apartments. Broke-down basketball hoops. We see little kids just sitting around looking at us.

Now we're walking in the parking lot where they play loud music in the summertime. Little trees growing up in the concrete cracks. See a trash Dumpster and graffiti. See an airplane overhead. A bum walking down the street. We're walking through the ghetto. Our neighborhood.

*   *   *   *   *

Let me see. . . . First of all, I'm thirteen, but a lot of people think by the way I carry myself that I'm above my age. I'm an active person—I play football, basketball, and

---

[1]Ida Bees, or Ida B. Wells: a public housing development in Chicago.

baseball. I'm a good student—I have a 9.4 grade level in reading. But most of all I talk a lot (as you can see, or else I wouldn't be doing this!).

I live in a house right around the corner from the Ida B. Wells. My grandmother, June Marie Jones, moved into the house back in 1937, and she's still here. We all live here—my grandmother, my grandfather, Gusie Jones, my mother (who's also named June but we call her Tootchie), my older sister, Janell, and her baby, Muckie, my younger sister, Jeri, and my cousin, Jermaine. My grandmother has custody of me and my sisters because my mother has a mental illness. . . .

[Now] I'm talking to you from my bedroom. Really it's the living room and my bedroom. I ain't got no room—I sleep right here on this couch every night—and I'm fourteen almost. My mother is lying on the floor next to me on her little box spring, and my little sister's lying on the floor too.

I just interviewed my mom. She told me a lot of things about my father. It don't bother me. There's a lot of people out there without their own fathers. I ain't the only one. There's a couple of hundred thousand billion people around the world who don't know their fathers!

Let's see. . . . Went over to Lloyd's house after school today. We were watching this movie about this boy who was a booster. He got hit by a car and it knocked him out and he went back to slavery times. Back then the master beat you if you started to learn to read and write. This boy already knew, but he had to work in the cotton fields and pretend that he didn't. It made Lloyd's sister so angry and sad that she just started crying. That's why we have to fight for our education—because back then we had to fight and die just to read and write!

To me, black people are just more friendly than white people. I see this every day on talk shows. You see a Ku Klux Klan man and a black man. The Ku Klux Klan man hates the black man's guts. But the black man always says, "I forgive you, man. I forgive you for your sins." But I'm not gonna stereotype the whole white race just for a few bigots. I know all white people can't be bad, 'cause God made us equal. We all of us human. We all got red blood. That's all for tonight. Signing off. Peace.

*   *   *   *   *

My older sister, Janell, is seventeen and lives in the room right across from my grandma. She has a little two-year-old baby named Jhery Marquis Jones, who we all call Muckie. Everybody in the house is worried about Janell. She's been messing up a lot lately. Just last week she drank so much E&J that she almost died—they had to take her to the hospital!

The way I see it, what's happening with Janell is like what's happened to a lot of kids in the neighborhood. A lot of times the girl who people say, "This is going to be the kid that makes it," is the first one to have babies. Or the boy who's into his books all day—all he really wants is to be "with it," so when he gets the opportunity he's going to do all kinds of bad stuff. But the kids that have always been doing bad stuff are going to be the ones to go to school, because they're already tired of living that way.

My sister is just like those "good" kids. She was in the spelling bee, she was in the Academic Olympics, she was the salutatorian of her class. Then she started hanging with these girls—their house was filthy, they were filthy—and they just kept dragging her down and down and down. She had a baby, started staying out of school, started coming home late. But she chose her own path—let her walk it. Eventually she's gonna see it ain't the right way.

I interviewed Janell in our front room:

Hey, Janell! Come here! Can I interview you?
Janell: I don't care.

Hello, this is LeAlan Jones, sitting on the couch. It is 11:20. I'm gonna interview my sister, Janell Jones. Janell, tell me about yourself.
Well, I'm about five feet five in height. I weigh 116 pounds. I'm very fair-skinned. Um. . . . I'm very energetic, I like to have a lot of fun. . . .

Like to drink a lot. . . .
No, I don't.

Yes, you do. You smoke marijuana?
No, I don't.

Yes, you do! Tell the truth!
No, I don't!

Ummm. . . . Let me see. . . . You're seventeen?
Yes.

Have a child?
Yes.

How would your life be if your son wasn't here?
I probably would still be going to school. But I'm not saying that I regret having him, because I'd do it all over again. He's the most precious thing in my life. I love everybody in my family, but my baby is the most important thing to me right now.

When did you have him?
October the 10th, 1990.

Why did you name him Jhery Marquis Jones?
I don't know. . . . I guess Jeri was my little sister's name, so I changed the spelling for his name. And Marquis, I got that from my uncle Larry's car—he had a Grand Marquis.

By whom did you have this child?
Frankie Anderson.

How old was he at the time?
Sixteen.

What does he do for a living?
He doesn't have a job, if that's what you're asking.

What does he do?
I don't know what he do!

O.K. Where does Muckie's father live?
In the Ida B. Wells.

How did you meet him?
I used to go with a boy who was on the same basketball team that he was on. His name was Jermaine.

The one who got shot in the head?
Yeah. Jermaine got killed the same year I had my baby.

How did you feel about that?
I was sad. I was crying on the bus on the way home from the funeral.

How many close friends of yours have got killed through the years?
I don't know. I can't count all of 'em. . . . It's been a lot, though.

Could you name a few?
Like I said, Jermaine. And Yuk. Slick. Meatball. Cheezy and Vell. Shawn and Kenny. There's been a lot of people.

Would you say twenty-five?
Probably more than that. . . .

You think it was around fifty?
I don't think it was that many.

But around thirty or forty?
Probably somewhere in that area.

How do you feel about all these deaths when you just sit around and think about it?
Well, I know I didn't do nothing to nobody to make them do something to me, so I don't really have to worry too much.

For all the kids in America, what would you say to them about this?
About what? About killing? Well, there's a lot of people out there whose mommas just don't care. They don't give them money for nothing, and I feel if they have to sell drugs to get stuff that they need then they should be able to go ahead and do it. Now, I don't think it's right for them to go kill nobody, but I *do* think that the kids out there selling drugs should be able to do something to get them a little extra

money. Because some of them might be too young to get a regular job at McDonald's. So that's what I think. . . .

Me and my friend Lloyd Newman just did a description of our life for a week, and we want to give you kids in America a message: Don't look at ghetto kids as different. You might not want to invite us to your parties, you might think we'll rob you blind when you got your back turned. But don't look at us like that. Don't look at us like we're an alien or an android or an animal or something. We have a hard life, but we're sensitive. Ghetto kids are not a different breed—we're human.

Some people might say, "That boy don't know what he's talkin' about!" But I know what I'm talking about. I'm dealing from the heart because I've been dealing with this for thirteen years. These are my final words, but you'll be hearing from me again, 'cause I'm an up-and-rising activist. Peace out.

Response and Analysis

1. LeAlan Jones and Lloyd Newman say that, "if you play childish games in the ghetto, you're gonna find a childish bullet in your childish brain." What must a child know to survive in a ghetto neighborhood? What types of attitudes and behaviors do children living in such an environment develop to survive? How do these attitudes and behaviors differ from those held by children living in the suburbs?

2. Jones's sister Janell had a baby and dropped out of high school. When the baby was conceived, the father of her child was sixteen years old, and Janell was even younger. What factors best predict whether teens of this age will decide to engage in sex?

3. What factors influence whether an adolescent who lives in an environment similar to Jones's and Newman's will develop into a socially productive and happy adult? Why?

Research

Suppose that a local school system is trying to choose one of three new programs designed to reduce the number of pregnancies among teenagers. The programs differ in terms of how much emphasis is placed on encouraging abstinence, providing alternatives for handling coercive dating situations, and providing information about safe sex practices and contraception. The administrators have allowed parents to provide input into the selection of the program. Some parents believe that sex education is the responsibility of the family, not the school, and that there should not be any such program. Other parents want the program to emphasize abstinence and provide teens with a moral foundation for abstinence. Still others say that the program should emphasize modeling and role-playing to teach boys about gender sensitivity and girls about how best to handle pressure for sex in dating situations.

Suppose that you have been contacted to serve as a consultant. How would you advise the administrators and the parents about which program to select? Does research suggest that one of the programs might be more effective than another in reducing teen pregnancy? How might your values and those of the administrators and parents affect how you and they evaluate and select the programs? How might your values and those of the parents influence your and their evaluation of the program's success?

FLIGHT OF PASSAGE

Rinker Buck

Developmental Concepts
sibling relationships, father-son relationships, initiative,
individuation, independence

At fifteen and seventeen years of age, Rinker and Kern Buck became the youngest aviators to fly coast to coast across the United States. Their father, a former barnstorming pilot who taught them the romance of flying, was initially opposed to their trip. Proud of his sons' initiative, however, he relents. Over the next several months, the boys rebuilt a Piper Cub airplane on their own as they planned the journey. How would they get along on the trip? Would their personality differences clash? Here, Rinker Buck describes their relationship with their father and the envy and tension between Kern and him. As the journey unfolds, Rinker begins to recognize that the flight is more than an adventure; it is a way for the boys to prove their abilities to their father and to themselves. It also is a way for them to discover and express their love for each other.

We were just two boys, seventeen and fifteen, flying to California in an airplane built before either of us was born. Later that summer a reporter for the Associated Press would make us briefly famous by writing that we were the youngest aviators ever to fly America coast to coast, but it wasn't records or fame we were after. What we were really doing was proving ourselves to my father. . . .

As a boy, my older brother was private and shy, self-conscious about being small for his age. Kern was the classic oldest son of a strong, iron-willed father, secretly afraid that he couldn't live up to the model, and thus quite skittish and sensitive to criticism. Even his appearance suggested vulnerability. He had feathery auburn hair with red highlights, broad cheeks and trusting brown eyes that opened wide with disappointment when he was hurt. He mostly excelled at things that required a lot of solitude and a minimum of social contact, math and science, and his best friend was a science nerd and ham-radio freak who lived in the village nearby, Louie DeChiaro. . . .

Kern never developed a competitive instinct for sports and he was painfully bashful around girls. When he reached high school and decided that it was finally time for him to try a date, my sister Macky picked out the shyest girl in her class, scripted an entire phone conversation with her on a yellow legal pad, then held it up for Kern while he nervously dialed the number. . . .

I had watched my older brother play the role of diffident recluse and was determined to be exactly the opposite. I was the extrovert who was popular and did well in school, starred in the class play, and became captain of our undefeated soccer team. These achievements of mine were not based on merit, but instead on criminal behavior. I was popular because I was the class cutup, expert in such delicate and locally prized work as the cherry-bomb demolition of the school principal's mailbox, or the upgrading of the baseball coach's jockstrap with an invisible but medically effective layer of Atomic Balm. With me, trouble arrived in waves. . . .

My brother was miserable about this. He was shattered by the injustice of the world. He had behaved himself and followed all the rules and nobody seemed to notice whether or not he was even alive. I broke every rule and got all of the attention. He was terrified that I was either going to end up in prison, or become the President of the United States, outrageous behavior in a kid brother. More than anything in the world he longed for a quieter, understated younger brother who melted into the background and didn't upstage him all the time. *I* longed for a more outgoing, assertive older brother who could socially pave my way in school and act as a foil against my father. Meanwhile, I was mortified by the brother I had. Even the way Kern and Louie dressed—plaid shirts, clashing plaid dork shorts, black socks, and black hightops—drove me insane with embarrassment. . . .

My brother dumbfounded us with his plan on a Saturday afternoon in October. My father, Kern, and I were an inseparable threesome on weekends, and we were out in the back field chopping wood for my father's fire. . . .

That day, while my father and I split the wood, Kern worked ahead of us, sectioning the logs with a chain saw. Midway through the afternoon, Kern switched off the saw and dropped it to the ground.

When he looked at my father, Kern's face was cocked sideways and his chin was angled high.

This generally meant trouble. Kern disliked confrontation, especially with my father. He tended to hold important things in until the last moment. By then the idea burned so intensely inside him that he tended to argue his case more insistently than he had to.

"Dad," Kern said. "Rinky and I are going to fly the Cub out to California next summer."

My father put down his ax.

"Whoa. Say again?"

"Dad. Rinky and I are going to fly the Cub to California next summer."

"Ah Jeez Kern. Where'd ya get an idea like that?"

"From you Daddy. You."

"Me? I never said anything like that. I mean, a thing like this takes time. Lots of time."

"No Dad. I've thought it all out. We'll rebuild the Cub in the barn over the winter and fly it west next summer. Think about that Dad, just think about it! Rinky and I flying coast to coast."

"Now listen here, son. When I was your age I *worked* my way across, piecemeal, over four years. I didn't even get to Texas until I was almost twenty. Hell, I bet you don't even know what comes after Ohio."

"Illinois."

"Wrong. Indiana."

"Big deal Daddy. Big deal. Who cares about Indiana? You're just saying no to say no."

"Big deal! Is that what you say to your father? Big deal? Well listen here Kern, this is a big idea. It scares the bejesus out of me. Have you thought about money? Have you thought about the deserts? And what about the mountains? How the hell are you going to get a Piper Cub over the Rockies? What pass are you going to fly?"

Kern wasn't sure about that yet.

"See Dad? See? You always turn a conversation into a quiz. How do I know what pass to fly? I'll figure that out later."

Even though the pipe in his mouth was already lit, my father reached into the pocket of his work jacket for his spare and nervously tapped in some tobacco.

"Oh Christ Kern. Why do you do these things to me?"

"Dad, you can't say no. I *have* to do this thing. I mean . . . Dad, I've been dreaming about this for a long time."

"Kern, I'm not saying 'no.' I'm saying 'maybe.' And that's a big, fat 'maybe' too. I've got to check my thinking on this."

"Fine Dad. Do all the thinking you want. But I've already made up my mind. We're going."

Kern pulled the chain saw back to life and roared through another log.

I was annoyed that my brother had included me in his scheme without consulting me first. . . . We were very impulsive and barmy as a family and I was used to it by now. . . .

"Rink, I *need* you for this," my brother said. "I can't do it alone."

It was the most ludicrous idea I had ever heard. My brother barely had one hundred hours in his logbook. He had never piloted a plane beyond the Delaware River in Pennsylvania. Nobody flew a Piper Cub all the way to California. Nobody had even thought of it until my earnest, dreamy brother came along.

That fall, after Kern received his private pilot's license, we had flown a few times together, and I was surprised by how much we enjoyed ourselves in the air. Kern wasn't at all demanding like my father and, when he gave me the controls, he didn't mind the way I wallowed the plane around the sky. In fact, he was idiotically easy to please. All I had to do was sit in the backseat of the Cub and not complain while he "pulled a buzz job" over Louie DeChiaro's house, or pretend that I wasn't airsick when he threw a roll of toilet paper out the window and then screamed down through the clouds to slice up the unfurled rolls of paper with the prop. I wasn't doing anything back there, except turning green. But Kern was extravagantly grateful for my company and complimented me profusely on being a "great copilot."

Those flights revealed an important side of my brother to me. He was not only lonely, he was desperate for my approval. He didn't have a lot of close friends anyway, and those that he had didn't know a thing about aviation. I was the only one who knew what he was really like as a person, which to Kern at that age meant what he was like as a pilot. He enjoyed my company and wanted more of it, and I could tell that he was immensely frustrated by my failure to respond to him the way he felt a younger brother should. But it wasn't in Kern's nature to blame me for that, he blamed himself. Winning me over and earning my love was an enormous piece of unfinished business for him, another one of those things that he wanted out of the way and resolved before he left for college.

I was just fourteen that fall and in the throes of an awkward adolescence, and I was never going to admit that I experienced such nauseating emotions about my brother. I didn't want to talk about such things. So I assented to his plan, almost immediately, because if I didn't he would pester me endlessly about my obligations to him "as a brother." Besides, by then my teenage rebellion against my father was in full swing. I was still getting into trouble at school and my father and I fought a lot about that. Without really meaning to, Kern was finally doing what I had expected of him all along. His coast to coast plan, which would require a long winter rebuilding the plane in the barn, offered me a perfectly defensible excuse for dodging my father for almost a full year. . . .

The simple audacity of our trip, our complete naïveté and nonchalance, astounds me still. Our tiny, two-seat Cub, manufactured in 1946, had no battery, no radio, no lights, not even a starter. The four cylinder Continental engine was ignited by my brother yelling "Contact!" from the cockpit while I stood outside, swinging the propeller by hand. Our only navigational aids were an ancient magnetic compass bolted to the instrument panel and a shopping bag filled with airmen's charts. We nearly killed ourselves getting over the Rocky Mountains and, as we followed paved highways through the remote deserts of New Mexico and Arizona, the cars and pickup trucks traveling the blacktop the same way routinely overhauled us from behind and passed us, mocking us with their dust-devil wakes as they sped on west.

Most of all, we were naïve about ourselves. Setting out on our journey, my brother and I considered ourselves young adventurers in the style of the aviation greats—Wiley Post, Charles Lindbergh, Antoine de Saint-Exupéry. We would coax our frail plane across the continent, conquering every inch of terrain between New York and L.A., simply because "it was there." But this was bunk. In fact, we needed to discover each other as brothers. The love that had been bottled up inside us since we were boys had to be acknowledged and expressed somehow, and this was all we knew, flying. And there was redemption for us in the perils of a coast-to-coast flight. That is what we found out among unfamiliar deserts and high mountain passes, and that is what odyssey is all about I guess. The odyssey was us.

Research and Analysis

1. Is it unusual for two siblings to be as different from each other as are Rinker and Kern Buck? Why or why not? What might significant differences in personality among siblings suggest about the extent to which personality is shaped by family environment (especially by having the same parents)? What other factors might cause siblings' personalities to differ?

2. How was the Bucks' journey a way to "discover each other as brothers" and express the love between them? Why might it have been difficult for them to express their emotions for each other in another way? Is it common for boys to have difficulties expressing love for each other? Why or why not?

3. How did the way Rinker and Kern approached their adventure reflect individuation, identity development, and initiative?

4. Imagine you are these boys' father or mother. Would you have let the boys fly on their own across the United States? Why or why not? Why do you think that their father eventually gave his permission?

Research

Programs such as Outward Bound are designed to provide physical and mental challenges that require individual initiative and group cooperation. Suppose that you are interested in studying whether teenagers who participate in challenging activities gain self-confidence and improved social skills. To study this question, you need to compare a group of teens who participate in a program with a group of teens who do not. How would you ensure that the two groups are comparable in self-confidence and social skills before the study begins? On what variables should they be matched? How might you measure their self-confidence? Their social skills? How long after the experience would you measure these attributes?

Credits

Section 1 Birth, Infancy, and Toddlerhood

p. 3: Excerpts from *Madeleine's World: A Child's Journey from Birth to Age Three* by Brian Hall. Copyright © 1997 by Brian Hall. Reprinted by permission of Houghton Mifflin Company. All rights reserved. **p. 11:** Rigoberta Menchu, "Birth Ceremonies of the Quiche Community" from *I, Rigoberta Menchu* by Rigoberta Menchu, translated by Ann Wright. Copyright © 1984. Reprinted by permission of Verso UK. **p. 16:** From *The Earliest Relationship* by T. Berry Brazelton and Bertrand Cramer. Copyright © 1990 by T. Berry Brazelton, M.D. & Bertrand G. Cramer, M.D. Reprinted by permission of Perseus Books Publishers, a member of Perseus Books, L.L.C. **p. 20:** From *Parenting the Fussy Baby and the High-Need Child* by William Sears. Copyright © 1996 by William Sears and Martha Sears. Used by permission of Little, Brown and Company (Inc.). **p. 25:** From *Operating Instructions* by Anne Lamott. Copyright © 1993 by Anne Lamott. Reprinted by permission of Pantheon Books, a division of Random House, Inc.

Section 2 Early Childhood

p. 33: Excerpts from *Madeleine's World: A Child's Journey from Birth to Age Three* by Brian Hall. Copyright © 1997 by Brian Hall. Reprinted by permission of Houghton Mifflin Company. All rights reserved. **p. 38:** From *Mollie Is Three* by Vivian Gussin Paley. Copyright © 1986 by University of Chicago Press. Reprinted by permission. **p. 43:** Excerpted with permission of Simon & Schuster, Inc., from *Classic Crews: A Harry Crews Reader* by Harry Crews. Copyright © 1993 by Harry Crews. **p. 48:** Reprinted with the permission of Scribner, a division of Simon & Schuster, Inc., from *Angela's Ashes: A Memoir* by Frank McCourt. Copyright © 1996 by Frank McCourt. **p. 53:** Excerpts from *An American Childhood* by Annie Dillard. Copyright © 1987 by Annie Dillard. Reprinted by permission of HarperCollins Publishers, Inc. **p. 56:** Ann Colin, "Our ADD nightmare," *Parents* magazine, February 1997. Copyright © 1997 by Gruner + Jahr USA Publishing. Reprinted by permission.

Section 3 Middle Childhood

p. 66: From the book *Growing Up* by Russell Baker, copyright © 1985. Used with permission of NTC/Contemporary Publishing Group, Inc. **p. 70:** From *Loving Each One Best: A Caring and Practical Approach to Raising Siblings* by Nancy Samalin. Copyright © 1996 by Nancy Samalin. Used by permission of Bantam Books, a division of Random House, Inc. **p. 76:** From *Hunger of Memory* by Richard Rodriguez. Reprinted by permission of David R. Godine, Publisher, Inc. Copyright © 1982 by Richard Rodriguez. **p. 81:** From Dixon, *The Spatial Child*, Copyright © 1983. Courtesy of Charles C. Thomas, Publisher, Springfield, Illinois. **p. 85:** Excerpts from *An American Childhood* by Annie Dillard. Copyright © 1987 by Annie Dillard. Reprinted by permission of HarperCollins Publishers, Inc. **p. 88:** Excerpts from *The Optimistic Child*. Copyright © 1995 by Martin E. P. Seligman, Ph.D., Karen Reivich, M.A., Lisa Jaycox, Ph.D., and

Section 4 Adolescence

Name Index

Subject Index